Generative Grammar and
Linguistic Competence

Generative Grammar and Linguistic Competence

P. H. MATTHEWS

Professor of Linguistics, University of Reading

London
GEORGE ALLEN & UNWIN
Boston   Sydney

First published in 1979

GEORGE ALLEN & UNWIN LTD
40 Museum Street, London WC1A 1LU

© George Allen & Unwin (Publishers) Ltd, 1979

415
M441g

British Library Cataloguing in Publication Data

Matthews, Peter Hugoe
   Generative grammar and linguistic competence.
   1. Generative grammar
   I. Title
   415   P158

ISBN 0-04-410002-7

Typeset in 11 on 12 point Bembo by Bedford Typesetters Limited
and printed in Great Britain by
Biddles Ltd, Guildford, Surrey

PREFACE

This book began life as a series of lectures, given to undergraduates in their final year, from 1971/2 onwards. The first draft was written for private circulation, around 1974, to check that my arguments were in order. I have been greatly helped by comments received on that draft, in particular from W. Bellin, R. W. P. Brasington, D. Crystal, P. J. Fletcher, M. A. G. Garman, W. Haas, G. C. Lepschy, J. Lyons, F. R. Palmer, N. S. Prabhu, P. T. Trudgill, E. M. Uhlenbeck, Irene P. Warburton and H. C. Wekker.

I have now switched courses, and have seized the opportunity of a research fellowship, at the Netherlands Institute for Advanced Study in the Humanities and Social Sciences, to make a thorough revision. I am most grateful to the Dutch government for the leisure they have given me.

Wassenaar, Netherlands
February 1978

CONTENTS

A linguist who could not devise a better grammar than is present in any speaker's brain ought to try another trade.

Householder [1], p. 100.

§1. It is the measure of a scholar's achievement that other and lesser scholars should produce whole books debating aspects of his thought. What follows will, I hope, be understood as a compliment to Chomsky in that sense. It is certainly so intended.

§2. As a theorist, Chomsky has made important contributions on two levels.

Firstly, he has tried to clarify the subject matter of linguistics. On this level, the key notions are those of a generative grammar and of the speaker's linguistic competence. A particular grammar is seen as a description of, or a theory about, the competence of speakers of a particular language. A theory of grammar is seen as a theory about the form of linguistic competence in general.

Secondly, he has put forward a specific theory of grammar, or a succession of related theories, conceived in such terms. On this level, the key notions are those of deep and surface structure, of grammatical transformations, and so on.

On a third level, Chomsky has also made important contributions as an English grammarian: for example, in distinguishing patterns with infinitives. (Thus the construction of *I persuaded* – versus *I expected* – *the doctor to examine him.*)

A critic must keep these levels separate. Perhaps it is wrong to distinguish such patterns; but the theory of transformations need not be impugned. Or perhaps it is right; but the distinction could be made in grammars without transformations, or which are not generative (for example, in a reference grammar such as that of Quirk and his colleagues [2]). We might reject transformations, but accept Chomsky's account of our goals. We might disagree on goals, but still formulate transformations.

In the past some scholars have looked on Chomsky's theories as a package. A critic might be expected to deal at once with the formal concept of grammar and, for example, with generative phonology. (See a review by Lakoff of Hockett's *The State of the Art* [3, 4].) This was understandable; for at that time most linguists either agreed or disagreed with Chomsky on all points. But the package can be split up, as divisions among his followers have now made plain.

§3. This book deals with the first level only: in particular with the key terms in its title.

According to Chomsky, a speaker has *internalised* the rules of a generative grammar. This is his account of what it means to know a language. I will argue that the account is unconvincing. In that respect I would agree in part with certain generative semanticists: for example, with McCawley's important review of Chomsky's *Studies on Semantics in Generative Grammar* [5, 6].

But we need not conclude that generative grammars are invalid. A grammar is a partial description of a language; it tells us, in certain terms and within certain limits, what the language is like. One way of telling us is to characterise a set of sentences. In writing a generative grammar we are simply writing a type of grammar which does this.

A grammatical theory specifies the terms in which a particular grammar is written. Let us assume that the same terms should apply to all grammars; then it can be seen as a hypothesis about the features which all languages have in common. Just as a generative grammar is one type of grammar, so a theory of generative grammar is simply one type of grammatical theory.

This says nothing about a generative grammar in the speaker's mind, or a theory of generative grammar in the minds of infants. As grammarians we are not concerned with such issues. Our business is with problems that arise in the investigation of languages. The nature of linguistic competence is the topic of another investigation, for which we wear another hat.

§4. Let us imagine that I am reading this to a group of colleagues. I fear that at this point I may suffer my first interruption.

"But how *can* these topics be separated? Linguistics is a science, and a grammar is itself a scientific theory. Chomsky has shown us what it is a theory of – namely, of the speaker's competence. He has also shown what form a grammar must take to qualify as such a theory – namely, it must be a generative grammar. That is precisely what such grammars are. A generative grammar is, by definition, a theory of the speaker's competence."

This comment would not be surprising, especially from a younger linguist, whose studies may have begun with Chomsky's *Aspects of the Theory of Syntax* [7]. But that is not the basic definition. By a generative grammar we mean a set of rules which characterises a set of sentences. That is all it meant in Chomsky's earlier writings, including *Syntactic Structures* [8].

We may distinguish three senses of this term. Basically it designates a type of formal system; let us call this a generative grammar in sense 1. The term is then transferred from the system to its interpretation; so, a theory of the speaker's competence is a generative grammar in sense 2. Finally, it is transferred from the theory to its object; so, the speaker has internalised a generative grammar in sense 3. Between senses 2 and 3 there is an acknowledged ambiguity – the 'systematic ambiguity' of Chomsky's *Aspects* [7], p. 25. But senses 1 and 2 must also be separated, the system itself being independent of its application to a putative object.

I am disputing Chomsky's account of what a grammarian is doing. Grammarians are not concerned with generative grammars in sense 2, or theories about a generative grammar in sense 3. They simply describe languages. But in doing so, they may formulate a generative grammar in sense 1.

§5. I fear some hecklers will not be satisfied.

"But linguistics is a science, as I said. As scientists we adopt a hypothetico-deductive method, proposing theories about some object. So to what object are linguistic data relevant? There is no entity 'the language', existing independently of the community that speaks it. What exists are the speakers; their minds are the only object about which a scientific grammar can be formulated."

Such reasoning is the curse of twentieth-century linguistics. We assume that our subject is, or must be, a science. We then look to the philosophy of science, or whatever philosophy of science is in mode, to find out what such subjects are. There was once a fashion for reductionism; so linguistics had to be limited to observables.

There has since been a rage for the hypothetico-deductive method, especially as a model for the physical sciences. So, we try to make linguistics look like our conception of physics or of chemistry.

"But are you denying that it is a science?"

It is not my business to decide how we should use this term. But that a grammarian practises a science in the sense that the objector intends – yes, of course I deny it.

§6. In writing a grammar we are giving information about a language. So too, for instance, if we write a dictionary. Then is lexicography another such science?

Let us imagine a fool who thought that it was. The *Oxford English Dictionary* is 'on historical principles'; so, he sees it as a theory of the competence of ideal speaker-hearers, as it has historically developed. ('But of course it is quite unformalised. Its entries have never been tested by the hypothetico-deductive method.') A bilingual dictionary he might see as a theory about the competence of an ideal bilingual. Such nonsense would at once be recognised for what it is.

Yet dictionaries are open to evaluation. We find a definition clear or unclear, right or wrong, to the point or full of irrelevancies. We find that a dictionary is comprehensive, or that words and senses are unjustifiably omitted. We may even use the word 'scientific': thus a dictionary is or is not constructed on scientific principles.

This last remark has nothing to do with natural science. Nor has the notion of a scientific grammar.

§7. Other colleagues might adopt a kindlier view.

"But naturally there are other goals besides the one which Chomsky has proposed. One is the writing of dictionaries, in part for practical use. There are also practical grammars, and taxonomic grammars for descriptive ends. But all this shows is that different people want to do different things. A molecular biologist does not object to botany on the grounds that it is not molecular biology; he sees them as different subdisciplines. Likewise there are divers goals within linguistics. Both sides must live and let live."

First, I did not say that grammars were necessarily what you call taxonomic . . .

"OK, then you are proposing another goal for generative grammars. Our goal is to understand the nature of a speaker's competence, or of the human faculty of language in general. We argue that this is comparable to the aims of other sciences. You suggest another, perhaps more modest aim, which perhaps is scientific in some other, perhaps more popular sense. Again, let us live and let live."

It seems churlish to disagree with someone so reasonable. But, like him, I am interested both in particular languages and in the general understanding of a speaker's ability. So far we have the same goals. But I think it is confusing to treat both at once. At one level grammars are the central topic: we assess alternative concepts of a grammar (thus of a generative grammar in sense 1, or of a grammar which our generativist would call taxonomic); also the merits of particular types, such as a grammar with or without transformations. We will not see these issues clearly unless we free our minds from thoughts of the speaker's competence.

On the other level we will see clearly only if we free our minds from thoughts of grammars. A grammarian tries to make precise and general statements, whose field of application is clear-cut. We have no reason to assume that speakers know their equivalent.

"Nor have we any reason, *prima facie*, to believe not."

Of course, this is something about which we might argue. But if we define a grammar as a theory of the speaker's competence (§4, sense 2), requiring of it a refinement of the properties traditionally found in grammars (ibid., sense 1), and then ascribe this theory to the speaker himself (ibid., sense 3), all scope for argument is closed.

Let us think again about the analogy with biological sciences. A man might work both in botany and in molecular biology, or work in one and take an active interest in the other. But he would not pretend that they are the same field. Likewise one may write grammars, or propose grammatical theories, and take an interest in theories of linguistic competence. But we must keep these theories separate; if not, each investigation will mess up the other.

§8. Let us try another analogy, which may perhaps be more helpful.

In *Linguistic Form* Bazell compares the description of a language to the mapping of a country: it is, he says, 'an affair of cutting and smoothing'. 'The problem', he adds, 'is where to cut, and where to smooth' ([9], p. 93). Describing a language is again what I call writing a grammar.

Now, of course, a grammar is not a map in any literal sense. What is the terrain that we could say it covered? But maps do have important properties that grammars also have.

First, there is the obvious problem of selection. In Britain the Ordnance Survey maps distinguish high ground and low ground but not, for example, grassy slopes and scree. These are maps for general purposes: a motoring map may not distinguish high and low ground either. A grammarian, in turn, may distinguish forms in regional but not in social dialects. He might, indeed, say nothing about dialects at all. Only a fool would object in principle to such decisions. (We will meet such a fool in §63.)

We also cut and smooth in representing what we do choose to represent. The map shows a contour line from A to B. But is the ground exactly that height all the way along it? Most likely not: there will be bumps at one place and depressions at another. The grammar has a rule excluding x in such and such constructions. Does that mean that the grammarian has never heard it? No, not necessarily. Again, it is only fools who would object to such operations.

Nor does a map deal with geological theory. Why is there a lake in Cwm Idwal in Caernarvonshire? We know why: it is a classic effect of glaciation. But this is not something we expect a map to tell us. What is the nature of the San Andreas fault in California? Here our knowledge has altered radically in the past ten years. But does that mean that we must change our atlases? No, of course not.

Likewise a grammar does not seek to explain the nature of language. Nor is it any part of such an explanation. A man who thought that it was would be like a man who thinks that a map is part of an explanation of erosion or of plate tectonics.

§9. A user may assess a map, just as he may assess a dictionary. (I am again speaking to more rabid hecklers, as in §§4–6.) He may say that it is clear or unclear, that it gives too little or too much information, that it gives information of the right or the wrong sort, that it is accurate or prone to error. Again we expect an atlas, or an Ordnance Survey, to be prepared scientifically. But this does not mean that a map is a scientific theory, proposed and tested on Popperian lines. Indeed, what object could it be a theory of?

"Perhaps it is a theory about the ideal traveller's knowledge of the terrain."

I doubt if any colleague who said that would be heard seriously. Just as we take a commonsense view of maps so I invite my hecklers to take a commonsense view of grammars.

§10. Analogies can be no more than suggestive. To accept my thesis (§3) a reader must be convinced on two points.

He must agree that generative treatments can advance our study of particular languages. (So, that it is instructive, or can be instructive, to formulate rules distinguishing sentences from non-sentences.) If the theory of competence is bathwater, he will agree that there is a baby which should not be thrown out with it.

He must then agree that the properties of generative grammars are not those of a grammar internalised by speakers. This wording allows for varying opinions. To me it means nothing to say that grammars are internalised Others may see the metaphor as harmless, deny that a speaker's grammar is like a grammarian's grammar. This is the sense of the remark by Householder which I have put at the head of this discussion; perhaps I could also refer to my contemporary review of *Aspects* [10].

Indeed the thesis is not new. I return to it because, on these points as for Chomsky's theories in general (§2), it may now be easier to separate the issues.

§11. I assume that my job is to argue against Chomsky's supporters, not my fellow critics. We can therefore take the first point rather briefly.

Of the grammatical work which generativists have done, much is disappointing. Sometimes things are wrong when the tradition has them right. Sometimes a tradition is wrong and a generative grammar fails to correct it. Often a generalisation is given in the face of blatant exceptions. On such experience, some scholars see the whole approach as suspect.

"But all this shows is that there are bad grammarians, of our school as of others."

You take the words from my mouth.

"And suppose that a rule is wrong. Only by stating it precisely, and testing its consequences, do we find this out. In testing we envisage other rules with which it interacts: for example, a rule for the passive interacts with rules for the structure of auxiliaries. That is the great virtue of the generative method. In attacking our rules our critics are themselves employing it."

Quite so. I would add that many of Chomsky's school do not themselves employ it. We cannot judge the writing of generative grammars by the work of scholars whose deep structures are, in this sense, both untested and untestable.

§12. A generative treatment is, or can be, of descriptive value; on this my friend and I agree. But other treatments have their value too.

Let us return to the analogy of maps. In one map a range of mountains may be drawn in as a series of hillocks.

This shows a valley between spurs; we see clearly where the land is mountainous and where not, and what shape the valley has. But other things are obscured. We are told little about heights, and that only relatively. Indeed, we might be misled. Perhaps the head of the valley is higher than the ends of the spurs.

Another map will draw contour lines, say with colour shading.

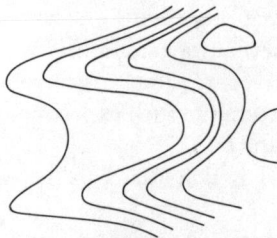

This gives us good information about heights, both relative and absolute. But the structure of the land will not be shown so clearly: for example, we may not grasp how deep the valley is. Each map has its uses and its limitations.

It is the same with grammars. Some grammars set out rules for inflections: for the Latin verb one rule will tell us that 3rd singulars have the ending -*t*, another that the first conjugation has an imperfect indicative in -*bā*-, a third that vowels are short before certain final consonants. The form *amābat* might perhaps be given as an isolated illustration. Other grammars set out paradigms: *amābat* will be opposed directly to *amābam*, *amat*, and so on. But the ending -*bat* or -*ābat* will remain unanalysed. Each form of statement obscures what the other is designed to bring out.

There are further parallels in syntax. To many grammarians generative rules are too particular: they give no general picture of the structure of clauses, of the order of words in noun phrases, and so on. But this is the price we have to pay for specifying sentences in detail. Another grammar sets out general patterns: for example, the tagmemic formulae of Pike or Longacre [11]. These will mislead us as to detailed combinations. But that is the price we pay for structural clarity.

"But surely the patterns are implicit in the rules. Given the latter we could derive the former from them."

I too have had this delusion: see my article on paradigms written twelve years ago [12]. But consider the pattern SPCA (Subject, Predicator, Complement, Adjunct). This is no more implicit in the base component of *Aspects* [7] than our map with hillocks is implicit in our map with contours. What tells us to ignore auxiliaries, or to lump together adjuncts inside and outside the verb phrase? Nevertheless both treatments are illuminating.

§13. A generative treatment also has heuristic value. We try to divide grammatical from ungrammatical: to do so we are forced to set up new constituents, and to distinguish new constructions. (Thus Chomsky's re-analysis of English auxiliaries, in *Syntactic Structures* [8]; even Joos comments favourably on this. Or the distinction among adverbials just referred to.) We will also find new problems, which we did not know existed. In this way our account of English, especially, has been much advanced.

"Yes, and that is precisely what we mean by hypothetico-deductive method. Our rules form a theory; we deduce consequences from them; we test if these are correct; if not, we see if another theory will do better."

But I am talking about heuristic method . . .

"Good God! Are you still after a discovery procedure?"

In an algorithmic sense, of course not. But I am concerned with ways in which a grammar is established and got right, not with mere confirming or falsifying. Some ways were codified by earlier structural schools: those involving contrast, commutation, and so on. But they are less applicable to syntax. In that field it is Chomsky who has done most to set us on the right track.

Alas, there was so much flannel about discovery procedures that only his critics seem able to see his contribution in that light.

§14. "So not only are you trying to bring back structural linguistics, you are trying to make Chomsky into a structuralist too."

Some people think that a structuralist is anyone who rejects Chomsky's package (§2); with such ignoramuses I decline to waste words. But a true structuralist will find little comfort in this book. For many of its arguments do not apply to generative theories only. We will underline this when we come to questions of word meaning (§§111–112).

Structuralism is at bottom a technique. This is no disparagement, since it has led to major advances. But we should not believe its slogans. 'Une langue est un système où tout se tient' – if this is meant literally then I cannot accept it. A generativist also has his slogans; the earliest spoke of 'the set of all and only the sentences of a language'. That too should not be reified.

But if such slogans are wrong, nevertheless they are fruitful. That, in essence, is the first part of my thesis.

§15. The second part is that they are, indeed, wrong. But with the word 'wrong' we at once strike a problem. For in what sense would Chomsky's views be either wrong or right? What status does his theory of language have?

Is it an empirical theory? In that case we will argue from evidence: we must show, as a fact, that language, or the speaker's competence, is not as a generativist conceives it. Some scholars have tried to do so: for example, by citing well-known facts of language variation.

Or is it a philosophical theory? Then the facts may not be in dispute; but we will argue that its terms are not clear, that it reduces to absurdities, or in general that it leaves philosophical problems.

Such arguments are also in the literature: for example, on Chomsky's use of the word 'know'.

Our approach will vary as we proceed. Often we will begin with facts, or with an argument relying on linguistic judgement. (For example, we might show that the acceptability of sentences varies with the context.) Some readers may then feel that I have said enough. But our adversary need not deny the facts; instead he has some covering explanation. (Thus he would say that acceptability reflects factors other than grammaticality.) We must then ask if his explanation makes sense. (What, if anything, does he mean by 'grammaticality'?) Finally we are forced into arguments outside our discipline.

§16. Above all we will have difficulties over terms. They arise as soon as I try to state Chomsky's standpoint.

In §3 I was forced to use the term 'internalise' ('. . . a speaker has *internalised* . . . rules'). I wanted to say 'learned', since I am trying to talk in plain words. But to learn a rule is to learn it explicitly; plainly that is not what Chomsky intends. So I am forced to use this strange word 'internalise'. Its sense is one which Chomsky himself has invented (*OED, Supplement* [13], s.v., §b) and which I cannot understand. But if I do not use it I will at once be dismissed as a misrepresenter. My only expedient is to put it, as it were, in scare italics.

"Then you admit that your criticisms may be based on misunderstanding."

No, of course not. A misunderstanding is one thing; a failure to understand is quite another.

"But you admit that there are difficulties of communication. This is what our side has always felt, that if these blocks could be removed the argument would vanish. But somehow, there are people to whom we can never get our message across."

Such comments I am willing to take in good part. For they are characteristic of the sort of argument in which I think we are engaged. In the end my case is not that Chomsky's theory is false, but that it is incomprehensible.

§17. So much as a preliminary. Let us turn to substantive discussion.

The arguments which follow come from various sources, some within linguistics and some outside. Some I have already raised in previous papers and reviews. In that sense there is little that is basically new. But it is important that we should try and tie them together. For they are fragments of the *same* argument, implying a view of language which a generativist can understand as little as I understand him.

'LANGUAGE IS NOT WELL DEFINED'

§18. In formal linguistics, a system is well defined. We conceive of a vocabulary (V), the set of all strings over V (V*), and some subset L of V*. L we call a *language*. The members of L we call the *sentences* of L.

But has this anything to do with a real language (the English language, the French language, and so on)? When we speak in English, we can be said to utter sentences in English. But how could these form a precise set? Take these examples. *One and one make two. One and one and one make three. One and one and one and one and one and one and one and one and one and one make ten.* The first is a perfectly normal English sentence: we can readily imagine it being uttered. The third is a rather improbable English sentence: it is hard to see how anyone might say it. But we are only talking of what is normal or improbable. We have not sought a demarcation between sentences and non-sentences. Take the formula in general: One_1 *and* $one_2 \ldots$ *and* one_n *makes* n. There is no definite n for which this ceases to yield English sentences. So, the set of real sentences is *not* well defined.

Now a generative grammar is one sort of definition of a formal language. So, it would be an error to speak of a generative grammar of English, of French, and so on.

Such, as I understand it, was the basic argument of Hockett's book *The State of the Art* [4]. However, we must consider two possible replies.

§19. The first is that of, for example, Ardener in an ASA monograph, *Social Anthropology and Language* ([14], pp. lxv–lxvi).

In this view the formal language is a *model* – a well-defined model, albeit of an ill-defined object. We say that such and such a grammar generates the sentences of English. But this is not strictly so. In fact, it generates a set of formal sentences in just the sense referred to. These formal sentences are then interpreted as a model of what we called the real sentences.

Why should we make such models? The answer is simply that they are fruitful. This fits with what we said earlier (§13).

§20. But modelling, like mapping, is a technique in which we close our eyes to certain aspects of the phenomena. For instance, we might devise a model of traffic which ignores the size of vehicles; if that helps us to study traffic flow then well and good. A generative grammarian ignores certain aspects of real languages; naturally we must ask if this is also well and good.

For perhaps he is closing his eyes to something vital. That, certainly, was Hockett's view. He himself talks of 'the assumption' that a language is well defined. Any 'approximation' we can so achieve will be obtained, he says, 'by leaving out of account *just those properties of real languages that are most important*'. This is cited from the preface added to his monograph of 1967 [15], p. 10.

§21. Ardener's reply says nothing about a grammar in the speaker's head (what we have called a generative grammar in sense 3). That will not satisfy the colleagues who interrupted earlier.

"But Hockett is confusing competence and performance. The sentence is a unit of competence; it is characterised by rules which the speaker has internalised. These draw a clear distinction between sentences and non-sentences. But we cannot expect a clear line in performance. For other factors intervene.

"Let us take the same schema: *One$_1$ and one$_2$ ... and one$_n$ make n*. For any n, we say that the sentence is grammatical. If n is high there will indeed be obstacles to uttering it: the White Queen would need an aid to memory (she might record 'one's on an automatic counter) if she is to answer her own question. But that has nothing to do with the grammar which she has internalised."

Many writers make a terminological distinction between *sentences* and *utterances*. So, in this view, the set of sentences is well defined. But naturally there is no well-defined set of utterances. In Chomsky's terms, the notion of *grammaticality* is well defined, but not that of *acceptability*.

§22. That would be the second answer. But it is not clear why it should be thought convincing.

A generativist says that the speaker's mind controls an infinite set of sentences. But this is not a statement of observed fact. It is part of a theory; the sentence is a theoretical construct and its properties are theoretically specified.

So it is a good theory? Here we are given little help. To argue against it we must point to features of performance that it fails to account for. But how can we bring such arguments home? For our adversary always has these 'other factors' up his sleeve. We present what we imagine to be counter-evidence; 'OK', he says, 'but this may merely be a problem for the theory of performance.'

"But there are many cases where such an explanation does seem satisfactory. I am thinking here of Chomsky and Miller's account of centre embedding (see *Aspects* [7], pp. 12–15); also of work by Bever and his colleagues, such as his paper in *Advances in Psycholinguistics* [16]. And for Hockett's own example (*One and one and . . .*) the explanation is childishly obvious."

But suppose I present a case where it is not obvious. What answer will you give?

"Well, perhaps the explanation might not come immediately. But that does not mean that it cannot be found. Science is full of unsolved problems. We know that many questions can be answered in the theory of performance. We would surely hope that your case could be dealt with too."

No one can prove that such hopes are mistaken. Therefore the well-definedness of grammar could never be falsified.

§23. Plato's cave might have come into a generativist's mind. 'Hockett has turned his back to the sunlight; he is watching shadows. We are talking about the things that cast the shadows.' Hockett would have insisted that they are not shadows: 'No, what I see is the only thing that is real.' Neither gives us grounds on which we can continue the argument.

SYNTAX AND LEXICON

§24. "Well, if you want to argue perhaps you could begin by giving us some facts. You say there might be cases which suggest that grammars are ill defined . . ."

(Not quite what I said, but for the moment it will do.)

"Then could you please produce such cases?"

In my own review of Hockett [17] I thought it would be better to look at semi-productivity. For the term see Dik's critique of transformational-generative morphology [18]; also my own *Morphology* [19], ch. 12.

§25. In any language there are certain non-productive formations. Take the case of adjectives + *th*: *truth, warmth, depth*, and so on. New nouns cannot be created freely on this principle. In writing, *coolth* has been used from time to time (Supplement to *OED* [13]); its transparency confirms the morphological analysis. Yet it still seems queer.

A generative grammar has no trouble with this. The adjectives are marked with some syntactic feature ('+TH'), and a minor rule refers expressly to a '+TH' in the complex symbol.

Other formations are fully productive: for example, that of noun + *s* (the regular plural of *trunks, trees* or *rushes*) or verb + *ed*. Of course, there are exceptions (*mice* or *took*). But the productiveness can be confirmed by experiment: for example, Berko's experiments with children [20].

Here there is a major rule. Unless marked otherwise – unless there is some special feature in the complex symbol – any noun will form its plural so. Major rules abound in syntax. For example, there is the rule deriving adjectives + noun for any adjective and any noun. 'Any' again means 'any subject to exceptions'.

But many formations do not lend themselves to either treatment. Let us take three examples (repeating two from my earlier publications).

§26. Example 1. Various nouns can be converted to verbs taking object *that*-clauses: thus, *He* CABLED *that he would be arriving on*

Tuesday. Others cannot: thus *He LETTERED that . . .* But precisely which can and precisely which cannot? *He phoned that . . ., The ship radio'd that . . .*: either or both may seem acceptable. *He telegrammed that he would be arriving on Tuesday*: this is more acceptable than *lettered that*, but do we actually say it? *He minuted that . . .* (?), *The ship wirelessed that . . .* (?): I find *wirelessed that* worse than *radio'd that*, though I usually speak of 'the wireless' rather than 'the radio'. *The ship messaged that its position was so and so*: we may not like this, but it has occurred in an American news magazine. So is it really quite as bad as *lettered that*?

At what point do we draw the line between grammatical and ungrammatical? We could give an arbitrary answer: say, *minuted that, *wirelessed that, *messaged that.* But is there an answer we can justify? Why not asterisk *telegrammed that* as well? Or allow even *messaged that*, since we have an instance? The more evidence we get the more we will feel that there is no line to be drawn.

Yet a generative grammar has to draw one. Do we want a theory which obliges us to ask unanswerable questions?

§27. What rejoinder will my adversaries make? Perhaps it might be as follows.

"But in such an argument you are again appealing to the reader's judgement of acceptability. That is a property of (putative) utterances. But the issue is still one of grammaticality (§21). You are making just the same mistake as Hockett.

"Now let us consider an individual speaker (speaker A). He has internalised a generative grammar; so, his language is the set of sentences which it characterises. This set we can represent with a solid circle.

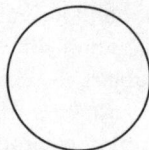

"Sentences within the circle are, we will say, 'grammatical for A'; those outside are 'ungrammatical for A'.

"However, there will also be other speakers (B, C, and so on)

whose languages are slightly different: these may be represented by
a larger broken circle

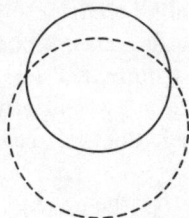

overlapping the first. A will regularly converse with some such
speakers. He will become familiar with their speech; he will thus
acquire a passive knowledge of their languages, in addition to his
own. We may say that he acquires a conception of their grammars.
Certain sentences, we may then say, are 'grammatical for A's conception of B's language', 'grammatical for A's conception of C's
language', and so on.

"It is for this reason, surely, that our judgements were so doubtful.
Telegrammed that is ungrammatical for some speakers; hence they
will not find it fully acceptable. But then it is grammatical for their
conception of the languages of some other speakers; hence it is not
fully unacceptable. We can image refinements. For example, *phoned
that* is ungrammatical for A, but many of his friends say it. *Messaged
that* is equally ungrammatical for A, but in this case very few of his
friends say it. In this way we could explain a gradation in A's judgements of acceptability."

We may call this the hypothesis of *idiolectal multilingualism*. We
will come back to it in the context of language variation (§76 and
following).

§28. Example 2. Nouns can be formed from adjectives by adding
-ness (*happy* + *ness* = *happiness*). But from precisely which adjectives? Let us take some colours. *Whiteness, blackness, blueness* – these
are certainly established English words. *Purpleness* – is this quite so
convincing? Compare *I admired the whiteness of his shirt, Cassius
envied the purpleness of his toga. Puceness, mauveness* – of course they
are intelligible, but would we actually use them? *Magentaness* (or
magenta-ness?) – this too is clear, but is there really such a word?
Eau-de-nilness – surely that at least is on the facetious side.

Which adjectives are to have the feature '+NESS' in their complex symbol? An ordinary dictionary will have to draw a line: thus nouns in -*ness* might be listed only if we have a written record of their use. But this is a matter of cutting and smoothing (§8). The formation is not closed in fact; we assume that new words of this sort can be created. Perhaps the dictionary will state this under -*ness* itself. Again the English language does not have precise bounds.

§29. There are two ways for the generativist to try and cope.

One is to insist that the speaker's competence is limited: say, *white* is '+NESS', but *magenta* not. Of course, someone might use *magentaness*, and we would understand it if we heard it. But this would be explained by a performance factor. Acceptability (of utterances) would thus extend beyond grammaticality (of sentences).

But why should acceptability be so extended? In our account of competence, adjective + *ness* is now on the same footing as adjective + *th*; but can *thickth* or *lukewarmth* serve as similar performance extensions? Compare *lukewarmth* and *lukewarmness*; do these strike us in the same way? Better still, compare *thickth* (*thick* being lexically '+NESS') with *warmness* (*warm* being '+TH'): are they equally acceptable? Why not?

"But naturally it depends on the size of the formations. The nouns in -*th* are very few, while those in -*ness* are very many. Obviously, it is more acceptable to extend a large formation than a small one."

That is not obvious at all. Fillmore ('On generativity' [21]) gives the example of *sit-in*, *talk-in*, and so on. Here we have a case of productivity from very small beginnings.

§30. In fact, it is not that horn of the dilemma that is usually grasped.

"Let us suppose, instead, that there is no limit in the speaker's competence. There is a major rule: for any adjective, adjective + *ness* is grammatical. But, of course, they may not all be actually used. That depends on quite extraneous factors. For example, eau-de-nil is not one of the basic colours; therefore speakers have not needed a noun to refer to it."

But why should this affect the issue? Adjective + *ness* is now on the same footing as attributive adjective + noun; why then should *magentaness* be awkward while *magenta paint* is not? *His face turned white, hers just turned eau-de-nil*: these are equally acceptable. *The whiteness of his face, the eau-de-nilness of hers*: these are not. Why, if all four are equally grammatical? What performance factor would explain it?

§31. Our generativist's first shift (§29) attempts to force this formation into the non-productive category; his second (§30), into the regularly productive. Each conceals a truth that the other expresses.

The beautifulness of his argument – perhaps *beautifulness* exists, but *beauty* would be much better. *The trueness of this proposition* – could we (or would we) say this? *Truth* is surely the established word. *The trueness of their friendship?* Yes; *truth* is not established in that sense. *The accurateness of his description, the rigidness of his views* – possibly we can accept these as alternatives to *accuracy* and *rigidity*. *I noticed the inaccuratenesses in his description* – but in this construction surely *inaccuracies* is preferable. *I noticed the loosenesses in his argument* – now it is the form in *-ness* that is itself the established word.

The barbarousness or *the barbarity of his treatment* – both words are familiar. *The brutalness* or *the brutality of his captors* – is there a word *brutalness*? (Think about it for a while. See if you can get used to it.)

We want to speak of well-established lexemes (*truth, accuracy, whiteness, looseness*). At the same time we also want to speak of a productive pattern (*accurateness, magentaness, brutalness, beautifulness* . . .). For the generativist this is paradoxical; we are trying to have our cake and eat it. But it is only his theory (the 'all and only' theory) that makes it so.

§32. Example 3. *A Rolls is very expensive, but you get a lot of car for your money*: the countable *car* is used (some grammarians will say) in an uncountable construction. Uncountables can also be used as countables. So how is a grammar to draw the line between them?

§33. Let us take a few examples which will set us thinking.

Lino isn't used much nowadays: lino, we say, is an uncountable. *Carpet is used a great deal*: is this acceptable? Put the two together: *Carpet is used much more than lino*. Are you sure that it is not acceptable?

Curtain is used a great deal: I think we will correct this to *curtaining*. (But did you think of *carpeting* for *carpet*?) *Cushion is used a great deal*,

table . . ., *bed* . . ., *settee* . . .: these are all at the countable pole.
Now let us add the quantification: *You get an awful lot of carpet for
your money*. In this frame *carpet* is entirely acceptable. *A lot of curtain
for your money*: do we insist on *curtaining* here? *An awful lot of
cushion* – well, why not?

A great deal of table? Of bed? (Please, not in that sense.) *Of settee?*
Do we accept these? They do not seem strictly normal.

But let us take a head noun which is more specific. *He looked at
me across a vast expanse of table*: now *table* seems uncountable too.
A vast expanse of bed? A vast expanse of settee? Let us suppose that
we are mice in a fairy tale; nevertheless *of eiderdown*, for example,
sounds better to my ear.

So, '*curtain* has the features + Count, — Mass' – yes or no?

§34. The problems of countability have been brought home to me
by Dr T. Monsen of Bergen. But most readers will be aware that
cases of this sort exist. Gradiences have been discussed by Quirk and
others since the mid-1960s: see his article in *Language* [22], also
Crystal's in the *Lingua* volume on *Word Classes* [23]. A similar point
has since occurred to Ross and possibly some other transformational
grammarians: see, for example, Ross's contribution to the 1972
Georgetown conference [24].

A grammarian should not abandon the notions of countability
and uncountability. As sorts of use they are quite clear-cut. Nor is
it improper to say that certain sorts of nouns 'are countable' or 'are
uncountable'. Fuzziness is not everything. But in addition there is
a tendency for countables to function as uncountables: some more
than others, some more strongly in specific frames. Who is to say
precisely where a tendency ends?

This is not the sort of question that a grammar (in the traditional
sense) has had to answer. It is a matter of the semantics of individual
words.

§35. There are at least two forms of creativity at work in ordinary
speech.

One is the creativity that is governed by rules. If there is a noun
wug there is a plural *wugs*. If we can say *The wug chortled* we can also
say *The wug didn't chortle, Did the wug chortle?*, and so on. This is
the creativity of syntax and inflectional morphology.

The other is governed by tendencies, by patterns of analogy. If we can talk of the 'core' of an apple then maybe we could talk of the 'core' of a carrot or a cabbage. (But we don't usually.) If there are 'headless men' then maybe we might speak of 'footless men' or 'noseless men'. (But are these really established adjectives?) If we can eat 'buttered toast' then why not 'rum-buttered toast'? This is the creativity of the lexicon.

'The lexicon is the set of irreducible irregularities' – Chomsky has merely taken over Bloomfield's maxim. Alas, it is a sadly impoverished view.

COMPETENCE

§36. "All right, so language is a little fuzzy. But fuzziness, as you say, is not everything. You mentioned Ross a moment or two ago. But Ross is himself a generative grammarian; he is one of many who are seeking to develop Chomsky's theory. Perhaps it should be developed in just the way you have suggested. That is, the speaker has a grammar and a lexicon which work on different principles. But this is a *new discovery* about the speaker's competence. You are contributing to Chomsky's theory, not attacking it."

This taunt will occur to some readers. But it is no more than a play on the words 'Chomsky's theory'. I have been arguing against the 'all and only' notion, as did Hockett (§18). My objector agrees that it might be wrong: for instance, that there might be no precise bound to some derivational formations. So a generative grammar in sense 2 (the supposed description of the speaker's competence) may no longer be a generative grammar in sense 1 (a well-defined system). He then turns round and says: 'Oh no! When I talk of Chomsky's theory I simply mean the notion of the speaker's competence.'

"OK, so I have shifted my ground. But you are arguing along lines which, as I say, have also been explored by some of Chomsky's disciples. Now they too are contributing, in a broad sense, to the study of the speaker's competence. So in reality are you; the only difference is that you seem unable to admit it."

At this point the argument becomes more scrappy. For the root problem is that I cannot grasp what my colleague means by the term 'competence'.

§37. "But this has been explained many times. If X is a speaker of English we say that he *knows* English: he knows that certain sentences are in the language, what meaning they have, and so on. X's competence is this knowledge of his language."

But I do not understand this notion of knowing a language. Granted, X can make a number of judgements; for instance, he might tell us that he would or he would not say such and such . . .

"In our terms, he would tell us that it is or is not acceptable."

In that sense he knows, or thinks he knows, whether it is in his language. But how could knowledge of that sort be said to govern his performance? Rather it is a reflection of it; it is *because* X is a speaker of English that such judgements are possible. This sort of knowledge is no more than a derived form of performance.

This last remark has gained some currency among American psychologists: see, for instance, Brown's *A First Language* [25], pp. 163*f*., 413.

§38. "Heavens! That is not what we mean at all. Look, let us talk instead of X's mental organisation. He speaks English – not French, not German, and so on. That means, his behaviour is controlled by a specific organisation of his mind. Our grammar is an account of this organisation."

But X behaves in all manner of ways. He says *Hullo!* and holds out his right hand; he sings Gilbert and Sullivan in his bath; he counts from one to ten on his fingers. Are these too controlled by this mental organisation?

"They are controlled by his mind, naturally. But not by his linguistic competence as such. Obviously, the mind has many different faculties."

We will have to return to this view of the mind. But for the moment our colleague is still begging questions. For why should we assume a separate faculty of grammar?

"Well, obviously, we cannot look into our minds to check that it exists. But let us simply talk of 'being a speaker of a language'. So, X is a speaker of English while Y is a speaker of French; there is a difference between them. Now, a generative grammar of English would be an account of what it means to be a speaker of English. Likewise a generative grammar of French is an account of what it means to be a speaker of French. In that way they explicate this difference."

At last we may be down to something we can begin to argue about.

§39. A generative grammar is part of a theory which accounts for X's performance as a speaker of English. But other factors intervene, as our colleague has already remarked in §21. What sorts of factors could we reasonably admit?

§40. One sort may be ascribed to human nature in general.

A speaker hiccoughs in the middle of an utterance. He might be speaking English or it might be French; the hiccough has got nothing to do with either. The same may hold in cases of hesitation. To establish this we would have to show that the incidence of pauses, 'er's, and so on could be predicted from general notions such as constituency or phrase boundaries.

Then there are Chomsky and Miller's remarks on centre embedding (see again *Aspects* [7], pp. 12–15). If they are right the effect should be the same whichever language is being spoken.

§41. Others will be ascribed to particular cultures.

Welshmen are apt to sing in situations where an Englishman would not. They are singing words; strictly, it is a difference in their linguistic performance. But it is not, it might be said, a matter of the English language and the Welsh language (or the English of the Home Counties and the English of Glamorgan). It is a non-linguistic difference between the peoples.

Again, a language L may have certain forms of verse or certain conventions of story telling. These, we might be told, are not part of what it means to be a speaker of L.

§42. Now let us think of two tribes, each with its own language. In tribe A it is considered manly to raise one's voice in speaking to women. In tribe B it is polite to speak to women very quietly. Is this part of what it means to be a speaker of A's language or of B's language?

Perhaps we will say it is. But then our generativist will have to handle it. Otherwise he will not account sufficiently for what it means to be a speaker of these languages. Would he accept that conclusion?

Or perhaps we will say it is not. But why not?

"Well, surely this too is a matter of the speaker's general culture." Why so? It is one of the basic parameters of speech that is affected.

"Well, yes. But it is not something that is governed by specifically grammatical factors."

But you are once more begging the question. What can we mean by these 'specifically grammatical factors'?

"But the practical grammarian has never found this any problem. It is not we alone who draw a line at this point."

Of course. This is an easy case of cutting and smoothing (§8). In drawing maps we distinguish churches with towers and churches with steeples; we do not distinguish tiled roofs and thatched roofs. That can certainly be justified. But then we do not pretend that we are explicating the character of a village.

§43. 'To be a speaker of language L': can we isolate precisely how we must behave in order to be one? No, why ever should we think so?

In tribe B men are expected to cover their heads in the company of women. They are expected to speak to women quietly. It would be rude to ask a woman for something with a certain intonational pattern. One does not use certain words in talking to women. Nor do women use them among themselves. Men distinguish a pair of pronouns, which may be translated 'he' and 'she'. So do women, but their forms are slightly different. A man can also use the women's forms in speaking to a sexual partner. Nor does he cover his head when he is alone with her.

Some of this is part of the language spoken by tribe B. Some is not. But how could we say precisely what is and precisely what is not?

§44. For real examples we may refer to Hymes's studies of 'communicative competence': see, for instance, his contribution to the ASA monograph mentioned earlier [26]. But Hymes's work may well suggest a way out, or what our adversary might think was a way out.

"All right, but a generative grammar (in sense 3) is only part of the speaker's competence. Let us assume that it is one thing he has internalised. This is his faculty of grammar, as we called it.

"But that alone does not give a complete account of what it means to be a speaker of the language. Therefore there must be other rules as well. These are the rules of his communicative competence, in Hymes's term. It is because X has internalised both sets of rules (both his grammatical and his communicative competence) that he is, in the fullest sense, a speaker of the language.

"Naturally, it is only the first set of rules that the generative grammarian is concerned with."

§45. Would Chomsky endorse this suggestion? In recent work he speaks of a *grammar* and, within it, a *core grammar*; beyond the grammar he seems to envisage some form of *pragmatic competence*. But I am not sure quite what he means.

For 'communicative competence' see also Wales and Campbell's chapter in the Penguin *New Horizons in Linguistics* [27]. But perhaps, again, this is not quite what they had in mind.

"Nevertheless, it is one attractive proposal. So what would you have against it?"

§46. Again, what reason have we for distinguishing these two sorts of competence?

"Well, we are linguists and Hymes, for instance, is an anthropologist. We are just distinguishing our separate fields. He is concerned with what he calls the ethnography of speaking. But this is a field that cannot, as you show, be separated from ethnography in general. We, as grammarians, do not want to get sucked into these problems."

Yet once more, we are not arguing as grammarians. We are arguing as theorists who are trying to explicate the notion 'speaker of a language'.

§47. Indeed I am not sure what the proposal would mean.

We are asked to postulate two sorts of rule. On the one hand there are *rules of grammar*. These are rules which would in part account for people's speech performance.

On the other hand there are (shall we say?) the *rules of speaking*. These are the rules that the ethnography of speaking would be said to investigate. Then what is their function? The answer, of course, is that they are rules which would in part account for people's speech performance.

So, we have two sets of rules both of which would in part account for people's speech performance. Why are they not just one set? Together they explain the speech in a specific language. Do we suppose that they explain it in different ways? Do we imagine that they make different contributions?

What different ways? What different contributions?

§48. We may be told that they account for different *aspects* of performance. On the other hand, there are the aspects that the generativist has been used to handling; these would be the province of the rules of grammar. On the other there are all the other aspects; these would be the province of the rules of speaking.

But is that a natural boundary? Let us look at two problems, both of which have often been mentioned.

§49. Problem 1. A generative grammar will have certain rules for intonation. *You're coming* is a statement with one intonation and a question (*You're coming?*) with another. Presumably the speaker will be said to have a rule by which one contour is derived from the 'Q' ('Question') formative. The other is then derivable when 'Q' is absent.

But *how much* intonation will be handled? Say *He's coming, is he?* On one tone this could be a straight request for confirmation; on another you are reacting to something you have just been told. With certain tones you may smile ominously: 'he' has a surprise coming. Without the smile it is again a simple question. You may heave a breathy sigh on part of the contour: 'he' is rather tiresome. With other modifications you may put up your fists. Such distinctions are well known; see, in particular, Crystal's detailed survey [28]. So what does the grammar account for and what not?

The problem is similar to that of §43 (behaviour of men and women in tribe B). But it cannot be shuffled off into communicative competence. For the boundary of communicative and grammatical competence is itself in question.

§50. Problem 2. A generative grammar concerns itself with

syntagmatic relations within sentences. *When I asked John he told me that he couldn't come*: we will normally take *John*, the first *he* and the second *he* as co-referent. The generativist will account for this in one way or another. One solution would have a syntactic rule rewriting *John* as *he* in two successive transformational cycles.

But similar connections hold across sentences. A. *I spoke to John yesterday*. B. *And I suppose he told you that he couldn't come*. Here A's *John* and B's *he* are again co-referent, but the rules of grammar (whether transformations or what) cannot relate them. Anaphora, we must apparently say, is governed by rules of speaking.

When I asked John she told me . . .: either John is a woman or some woman was chipping in. A. *I spoke to John yesterday*. B. *And she told you* . . . – this is interpreted no differently. Why should we believe that different sorts of rule are in play?

§51. Our generativist will perhaps talk of a distinction between sentence analysis and discourse analysis. But what exactly is its basis?

"But this is another distinction that is not ours alone. Surely all linguists have taken the status of the sentence for granted."

As a practical matter, yes. But as a matter of theory, no. Traditionally it has always been thought to need clarification. This is important, as Chomsky and his Bloomfieldian predecessors are among the few who have not worried about it.

§52. Could we extend the scope of rules of grammar? Would that be the answer to this second problem?

One suggestion is that the text and not the sentence should be taken as the basic unit. So, our speaker B would have internalised a characterisation of the set of possible conversations. As part of this there would be a transformation introducing *he*; its structure index might be satisfied by sentences, by parts of sentences, or by two or more successive sentences where necessary. So, in the example given, a rule of grammar would account for both the first and second *he* in B's interruption.

Would Chomsky, for one, accept this? I would have thought not. There are proposals for a 'text linguistics': see, for example, Dressler's introduction with that title [29]. But they cannot be taken so literally. Suppose that A and B converse for half an hour: are we to say that they perform an English conversation – one of a set of such objects generated by rules that they have internalised?

That merely reduces to absurdity the notion of performing a mental object.

§53. Could we instead restrict the scope of grammars, while extending that of rules of speaking? Some colleagues might suggest this.

"In the conversational fragment which you have given B did, admittedly, say *he* (*And he told you* . . .). But in another context he might well have said *And John told you* . . ., referring to the same behaviour on John's part. Why not in the actual context? The answer is that A might have misunderstood: he might have thought, for a moment, that some other John was meant. He therefore employed a rule of speaking by which *he* is substituted.

"Now let us turn to the single sentence (*John told you that he* . . .). Again, it would be grammatical with *John* repeated (*John told you that John* . . .). But again the hearer may misunderstand. So, again, the rule of speaking introduces *he* instead.

"In this way *he* (and similar pronouns) are eliminated from the grammar. But then they are supplied by the *same* rule of speaking, whether the co-reference is within or across sentence boundaries."

§54. There is a parallel here in Lyons's discussion of these issues: see in particular his *Semantics* [30], Vol. 2, pp. 586*ff*.

Lyons is talking of the linguist's idealisation of his subject matter. First we regularise our material: for example, to cut out any effects of hiccoughs. We also apply some standardisation, ignoring various forms of contextually determined variation. (We will return to this process in §63.) Our third step is one of *decontextualisation*, in which, for example, we restrict ourselves to the full form of sentences. Take another interchange: A. *Who did you see?* B. *John.* In this example the incomplete sentence *John* may be related to the complete *I saw John*: it is the latter, not the former, that is ordinarily the subject of our grammars.

Lyons is concerned with the grammarian, not the speaker; we are still cutting and smoothing. But consider the rule of ellipsis by which *John*, as a sentence, might be derived. On one view this might be a rule of grammar; perhaps it must again be a text grammar (§52).

But on another view this too has been internalised as a rule of speaking. So, the rules of grammar generate the full form *I saw John*; the ellipsis (*John*) is a matter of using *I saw John*, in an incomplete form, in certain contexts. That would correspond to the proposal in our last section.

§55. Would this (§§53–4) attract a hard-core generativist? I do not know. But as a critic I would still be puzzled.

A. *What's John doing over there?* B. *Picking primroses, I think.* Here B's utterance would be a performance (let us say) of the sentence *John is picking primroses, I think* (or even *I think that John is picking primroses?*). Presumably this is still derived within the grammar. But the rules are very similar: in each case *John* is erased (in the embedded clause, in the sentence B is performing) and the auxiliary complex is reduced. Why is one a rule of speaking while the other remains a rule of grammar? Here, as in §50, the reasoning is of a sort that generativists have happily used elsewhere: if we draw a distinction, and it prevents us from making a generalisation, then how is it justified? (For its use in this case compare Fillmore's paper in the 1972 Georgetown conference [31].)

I saw John, picking primroses I think: which sort of rule would be appropriate for this?

§56. I can imagine members of my audience who are getting thoroughly fed up with this discussion.

"Look, why are you pestering us on details? We have simply proposed a working hypothesis. We believe that the speaker has a competence that can be described by a generative grammar. Naturally, we believe that he has other rules as well. This is the paradigm within which we are working.

"Now, obviously, the scope of either set of rules must be a matter for empirical inquiry. There are many questions that we are not yet able to answer. But what does that prove? Merely that there is more work to be done! It has no bearing on the validity of our proposal. Why don't you shut up and help us with our empirical research?"

But I still do not see what, in principle, the grammar is about. What does it mean to 'know English' and then to have other rules which are concerned with 'speaking English'?

"But we do not need such verbal glosses. Look, a human being has a certain finite mental apparatus. Let us represent this by a solid rectangle.

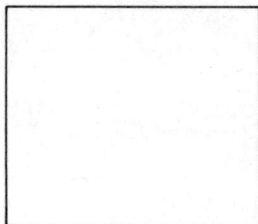

Part of this apparatus governs his behaviour as a speaker. Doubtless its boundaries are not so determinate (see again tribe B, §43). Let us therefore show it with a broken circle.

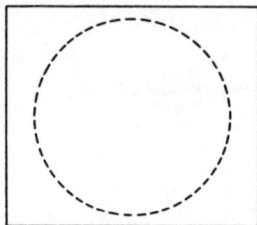

Some part of this, in turn, will be described by a generative grammar. We may show this with a smaller solid circle.

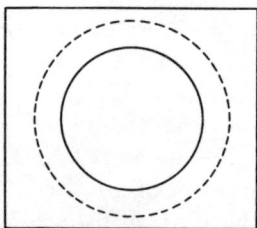

"There, that is all our hypothesis consists in. Now, have you really got any factual evidence against it?"

We will come back to such proposals in the context of sentence meaning (§§133 and following). But for the moment I cannot let this final question pass. For in what sense is it a testable hypothesis? What empirical evidence could one imaginably have against it?

VARIATION IN SPEECH COMMUNITIES

§57. A speaker is a member of a speech community. Thus I am in the same community as other speakers of southern British 'received pronunciation', or other speakers of standard English, or other English speakers generally. It is well known that such communities are heterogeneous. For example, two members may speak different regional dialects. We also know that any individual's speech is heterogeneous. For example, he may speak a regional dialect in some circumstances and a standard dialect in others. In different communities, many different types of variation can be found.

These are hackneyed observations. The facts are familiar to Chomsky, as to everyone else. But how does the generativist propose to account for the speakers' behaviour?

§58. Let us begin with a conventional model of a speech community. In the following diagram A, B, C, . . . are speakers: the thickness of the lines shows the extent of their linguistic contact.

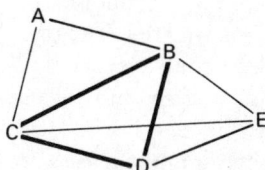

B, C and D talk to each other frequently; they form a cluster within the community. A and E do not talk to each other at all.

We can then look at certain features and determine how far they are shared. Each line shows one feature that is common to the speech of two individuals.

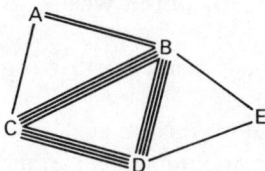

Again, B, C and D form a cluster. It is on this basis that we draw isoglosses, distinguish different dialects, and so on.

§59. The interest of this model lies less in what it says than in what it does not say.

What is said to be real? Only the individual speaker, his contact with other speakers, the associated similarities in their speech. But we are concerned with a community. I talk to all sorts of people; some are native speakers of my language, some are not. The community of native speakers of English – surely this, too, is real?

There are problems here for anyone who talks of grammars in the mind. For what minds can he talk of but the minds of individuals? 'La langue', as de Saussure made clear, is formed by a 'lien social' (*Cours* [32], p. 30). But where does this 'trésor' (loc. cit.) reside? 'C'est . . . un système grammatical existant virtuellement . . .', he says, 'dans les cerveaux d'un ensemble d'individus.' Here the 'ensemble' is crucial: 'car la langue n'est complète dans aucun, elle n'existe parfaitement que dans la masse'. But what is 'la masse'? One bad answer is to postulate a mind of something larger than the individual – a group mind furnished, we might say, with a group competence. Of course this is rubbish. But then it is only the individual 'cerveaux' that we are left with.

Am I raking over dead controversies? Indeed the point is an old one; it was already an issue between Paul and the social psychology of his day. But nonsense never quite lies down. What, for example, does Labov mean by the 'grammar of a speech community'? Of course, all grammars are of languages that are spoken by communities: we need hardly make a song and dance about that. But Labov is not referring to the linguist's description. His is a grammar in which, for example, changes are said to 'occur': 'the grammars in which linguistic change occurs are grammars of the speech community'. This is opposed to the view that changes are a matter of the individuals' grammars. But in what sense is Labov's grammar supposed to exist?

I am citing from the important article begun by Weinreich for the collection *Directions for Historical Linguistics* ([33], p. 188; see p. 97 for the authorship of this passage). In effect, Labov has taken over Chomsky's systematic ambiguity (§4) and made it much worse.

§60. "But could 'la langue' perhaps be the intersection of the individual speakers' competences?"

There seems nothing to encourage such a thesis. In §58 A's speech will be largely the same as B's, B's as C's, C's as D's, and so on. But that is all. Listen to some Devonshire farmhands. Then listen to a West Indian bus conductor. What is the common core uniting them as English speakers?

"But their grammars will have certain rules in common."

That is, we can write grammars (in particular transformational grammars) such that they will? No doubt we can. But we can do the same for English and French. Would we call such rules a characterisation of 'the Frenglish language'?

"But it is precisely because there is a French language and an English language that we have to look for such defining features."

Why should we suppose that they exist? Let us borrow an analogy from Wittgenstein ([34], §67): must a single piece of string have single fibres running from one end to the other?

§61. "Then could 'la langue' be the sum of the individual speakers' competences?"

But most communities do not have definite limits. How many Welshmen will we include as English speakers? Perhaps only some of them – but which?

"Those that have English as their primary language."

But what does it mean to 'have L as one's primary language'? To speak it more often than others? To speak it more in certain situations? To have learned it as one's 'first language'? But then what are the precise criteria for that?

Perhaps we will take it that all Welshmen are English speakers. In that case how many Indians, for example?

"But surely there is some difference between bilingualism and merely knowing a foreign language."

Indeed so. But we should not expect that every case falls neatly into either category.

§62. These are preliminary points, which merely need underlining. Our real problem concerns the 'features' (§58) which our individual speakers (A, B, C, . . .) are said to share or not share. What does this mean?

It is easy to slip into a naive view. A (we would say) calls such and such an object one thing, B another. B pronounces it with one vowel, E with a slightly different vowel. But we have already remarked that any person's speech is heterogeneous. I said in passing that my usual word was *wireless* and not *radio*; that is how I would answer a questionnaire. But that does not mean that I never use *radio*. In my speech, the *-ire-* of *wireless* would normally be monophthongal. But I cannot swear that I never use a triphthong.

Many variations can be related to contextual factors. Suppose that B is secretary to a local bank manager. In speaking to him (A) her vowels may be more like his, while in speaking to her sister (C) they will be more like hers. Examples abound in the literature on sociolinguistics.

What then is a linguist to do about such variations?

§63. As descriptive grammarians we can, if we choose, ignore them. This is a matter of standardisation, in the account by Lyons [30] already referred to (§54). Often we will be forced to talk of free variation. That means 'variation which we do not account for by the criteria of this investigation'. Sometimes it may indeed be random, but mostly not.

"But how *can* you ignore it? Heavens! When you get out and look at real speech data . . ."

Perhaps I may again answer by an analogy. Here we have part of a map. It shows a beach and some rocks in something like the Ordnance Survey system.

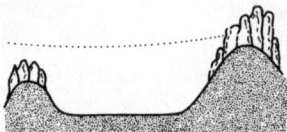

'But this is a picture of a beach that is so many yards wide. Heavens! If you go and stand there you will find the tide is coming in and out all day.' Surely that would be a very silly comment.

Alternatively, we could at least say how much variation there is. Or we might go further and enlarge in detail on some striking factor. Such choices are at bottom *ad hoc*. For beaches the Ordnance Survey does show the High Water Mark and Low Water Mark. It could show more: for example, the seasonal maximum and minimum for each. The reason for not doing so is that it would not in general help the user. Similar abstractions must be made in grammars.

§64. These are choices for the descriptive linguist. But our generativist denies himself such options. The variation is part of the speaker's performance, and cannot be ascribed to general factors, of the order of hiccoughs, memory limitations, and so on (§40). So how is his theory of competence to account for it?

We will look at two proposals. The first (§§65–75) is taken, or adapted, from one school of sociolinguists. The second, and more interesting, would apparently have Chomsky's own support (§76).

Variable Rules

§65. In the generativist's view, speech is controlled by rules. But usage is variable, not absolute; so, perhaps there are *variable rules* as well as, or instead of, absolute rules. By our first proposal, such rules are also part of the speaker's competence.

The sources must be identified with some care. Variable rules appear first in Labov's continuation of Weinreich [33]; they are the actual innovation in his grammar of a speech community (§59). He has since employed them in a number of interesting studies: on the use, for instance, of the copula in certain boys' gangs in New York [35]. So have others: we may pick out Wolfram's monograph on Puerto Rican English [36]. Perhaps the clearest theoretical discussion is in an article by Cedergren and Sankoff, dating from the same year [37].

The best of these studies deal with variation that is conditioned by the linguistic context (the type of clause, the phonological environment, and so on). With these I have no quarrel; they do not affect my argument. But the theory also covers non-linguistic factors, such as the class or profession of the speaker. It is that extension which concerns us.

§66. We can argue from a schematic illustration.

Let R be a rule in a generative grammar: say, a rule supplying a certain morpheme in a certain construction. We can say that a speaker 'uses R' if he utters a sentence in whose derivation R would play a part. But use of R may vary systematically. Let us suppose that older speakers use it less than younger, and those of higher classes less than those of lower. Let us also suppose that those of lower classes use it less when they are speaking to their social superiors. (Compare our secretary of §62.)

Now let V be the variable (we might call it the 'incidence variable') whose values are a function of these parameters. The speech of the community is then described (so far as this goes) not by R alone, but by R and V together.

A variable rule can be defined as a rule with which an incidence variable is associated.

§67. For descriptive purposes such rules are useful, at least in dealing with some types of variation. But what are the speakers supposed to have internalised?

Clearly R, for a start. In general, Labov talks of 'the speaker's knowledge of the language' just as Chomsky talks of it: for instance, in his study of the copula [35], p. 759.

But R alone does not account for their performance. A teenage labourer uses R (say) 90 per cent of the time; this too must reflect his competence. Our middle-aged bank manager has a usage of (say) 10 per cent; in that respect his competence is different. For Cedergren and Sankoff this reflects a difference in loading: in their terms, there is an 'input probability' in which 'a speaker's non-linguistic parameters (class, sex, age, etc.)' are incorporated ([37], p. 353). This is one of the ways in which they want to 'strengthen' the notion of competence (ibid., p. 352).

But that too is not enough. Our manager's secretary uses R with frequencies that also vary: perhaps 50 per cent at home, but 20 per cent at work. For a generativist this too reflects some factor in her mind. So, for Labov, her loading changes; in his terms, the 'variable input' may be governed by such factors as 'contextual style' ([35], p. 738). Like Cedergren and Sankoff, Labov presents his theory as an 'enlargement' of our current notions of linguistic competence (ibid., p. 736).

In brief, each speaker has internalised R. In addition, he has internalised some set of weightings (W) which will govern his use of R. The values of W will differ from one speaker to another.

§68. Now let us consider the notion of a speech community. By this proposal, speakers may be grouped on three levels.

They might have both the same rules $(R_1, R_2, \ldots)$ and the same sets of weightings $(W_1, W_2, \ldots)$; so, their competences are identical. A community of such speakers would be a speech community in the *ideal* sense.

They might have the same rules, but with partly different weightings; so, it is only their grammars that are identical. A community of speakers with the same grammar we may call a speech community in the *Labovian* sense. Examples might be the one he posited in his thesis [38], consisting of some but not all residents of New York City, or the Norwich speech community proposed by Trudgill [39].

They might communicate, but yet have partly different rules; so, not even their grammars are identical. A community of speakers who can talk together is a speech community in the *general* sense. For example, all speakers of English or specifically of American English.

A speech community in the general sense may not have precise limits (§61). But a Labovian community must; two speakers either have the same grammar, or they do not. So, a community in general is partitioned into Labovian communities (the speakers of New York English, of Norwich English, and so on), which might then contain communities in the ideal sense.

But this is instinctively wrong. Surely we know from dialectologists that a partitioning into dialects or sub-dialects cannot be justified.

§69. Let us imagine a change in progress. Some years ago the use of R was much less common; in the future it is likely to be used much more. This is a familiar topic of Labov's earlier work.

Then at what stage did the community internalise R?

Obviously, there was a time when they did not have it. That is, the morpheme never appeared in this construction. Then the change begins; the morpheme starts to appear in the speech of some younger members of the community. What exactly has happened?

Have all our speakers suddenly acquired R? But in that case why do only the youngest speakers use it?

"Well, obviously, we could posit that the older members have a nil weighting."

So, such a member has a set of rules which account for his speech, but one of these rules has no effect whatever on his speech. At one point in his life he did not use the rule because he did not have it; then at a later point he has it but he does not use it. That would be nonsense, surely.

"Well, perhaps for a while the younger speakers do have grammars different from their elders."

But that is merely to postpone the event. Suppose that there are speakers in their nineties who are still not using R at all: thus X, who is a retired bank manager. Then there are others of the same age who do use it: thus Y, who is a retired labourer. Are we to say that the community has acquired R, but X (unlike Y) is not a member of the community? Or are we to say that the community has not yet acquired it, but merely some members (such as Y)?

"But how could the community be said to exist as an entity distinct from its members?"

Quite so. This is in tune with our last section (§68). But it scarcely helps Labov. For he wants to take 'the community' as constant: this is the community in whose internalised grammar such changes are said to take place (§59).

§70. This first argument considers the extension of Labovian communities in time. Their extension in space gives rise to similar problems.

Let T be a county town; so, we might want to speak at least of 'the T speech community'. But all sorts of people live in T. Some were born and bred there. Some were brought up in the surrounding countryside, but moved to T when they left school. Some have come from a much greater distance, but have lived there a long time. Some have only recently moved in. These people all speak to each other. So are they all members of the T speech community?

In the Labovian sense, no. For his communities are defined, not by patterns of communication, but by having the same grammar. This we will call 'the T grammar'. So, some residents of T have internalised the T grammar; others have internalised different grammars.

Would this division be apparent from their speech? No, of course not. In usage there would simply be gradation, within and between the alleged communities. So, on what basis are their memberships to be investigated?

§71. "But there is other evidence besides that of their speech. Suppose X is a member of the T community. From the way Y talks, X will recognise that Y is also a member; he too is a 'T man'. Y will feel the same about X. From the way Z talks, both X and Y will recognise that he is not a T man. This will be so even when X and Y have very different usage.

"This shows that X and Y have common linguistic knowledge. It is that knowledge that constitutes the grammar of their community."

Such arguments were used by Trudgill in his work on Norwich. In Trudgill's words, the speakers 'share a common set of subjective attitudes' towards varieties of Norwich speech. They could also 'imitate without error', 'for humorous or other similar purposes', varieties 'other than those they normally use'. These quotations come from his paper to the 1972 Georgetown conference [40], p. 149.

So could this be our criterion? The T speech community, or the internalisation of the T grammar, would be co-extensive with these two abilities?

§72. But surely they are matters of degree. Nor do they always go together.

I was brought up in Devon and have subjective attitudes towards West Country speech. I remember when I moved to Reading from North Wales. The Berkshire dialect has West Country features; it made me feel much more at home. Now, suppose I meet a man from Totnes in the wastes of New York. I could place him socially far better than I could place the Americans around us. But I do not myself speak with a Devonshire accent. Nor have I ever done so. Nor can I mimic it with the remotest accuracy.

For that matter I have subjective attitudes towards Australian speech. These are shared by many other Englishmen. Then have I internalised rules which would allow me to speak that way?

"Yes, but because you are not in fact an Australian, you have internalised weightings which prevent you from doing so."

In charity, I will not try to give a reference for this suggestion.

§73. Now take the ability to imitate. Is it ever wholly without error? So, our bank manager could sit behind a curtain and convince anyone he was a labourer? Would this involve no special skill?

So, any member of the community could do it equally well?

"Perhaps not. But why should we expect it? Some speakers are more shy than others. Some have had more practice. Some, as you suggest, may have a special aptitude. Knowledge of the rules is only one factor."

Then is it a necessary factor? Some British speakers do imitate an Australian accent. Surely this comes from skill and practice only.

"Perhaps so."

Then we have no criterion. 'X has internalised rules enabling him to imitate the speech of Y'; 'X has a special aptitude enabling him to imitate the speech of Y' – how do we determine which is true?

§74. "But you cannot deny that these communities exist. In T the varieties of speech are such and such; in the next county, or in its county town S, they are different. It is only the boundary that is a problem."

Indeed so. But by this proposal it has to be precise. On the one hand there is the T speech community, all of whose members have internalised the T grammar. On the other hand, there is an S community, all of whom have internalised an S grammar. On what evidence do we draw a line between them?

"In practice, our data may naturally be indecisive. But in principle we could do it."

No, we could not. For once again we have two explanations for the same thing. In one, two speakers have the same grammar; nevertheless they speak differently. In the other they have different grammars; *therefore* they speak differently.

Let us image the line as a Labovian would imagine it. Some residents of T (A, B, . . .) are in the T community; the differences between their speech must be explained by different weightings of their variable rules. Others (C, . . .) are not; where their speech diverges it is because their rules are different. There is no qualitative difference in our evidence. Quantitatively A's speech could be closer to B's than to C's. (Think again of A as a bank manager and B as a labourer.) As in the case of change (§69), and of imitation (§73), our theory offers us one explanation too many.

§75. Labov has raised real problems of the individual and the community. For that we are indebted. But we will not solve them by 'strengthening' or 'enlarging' (§67) Chomsky's notion of the speaker's competence. Why not try abandoning it?

Idiolectal Multilingualism

§76. Let us return to the bank manager's secretary (§62). If she has not internalised a variable rule, then perhaps she has internalised alternative rules. Sometimes she uses one, sometimes another. These rules establish alternative grammars, generating slightly different sets of sentences. So, our secretary would be multilingual.

As Chomsky himself puts it:

> In the real world there are no homogeneous speech communities, and no doubt every speaker in fact controls several grammars, in the strict sense in which a grammar is a formal system meeting certain fixed conditions.

The passage is fairly recent, from a philosophical paper which appeared in 1975 [41], p. 318.

We have broached this notion before, in our discussion of *telegrammed that* and such-like (§27). But there the speaker's knowledge was partly passive; our secretary's grammars are all active.

§77. Consider an ordinary dialect and the way an ordinary dialectologist would describe it. One aim is to write a dialect grammar: a description of the speech in such and such a locality. But this must not be understood too literally. He will not get recordings of 'pure dialect'. There will be no informant using dialect forms and nothing else. Each individual's speech is heterogeneous, as we said.

Does that mean that a dialect grammar is an absurdity? Of course not. The dialectologist knows the standard language and knows something, at least, of neighbouring dialects. He can look at his data and say 'this form shows no appreciable interference from the standard', 'this is a standard form with only slight phonetic modifications', and so on. In that way he can abstract the dialect features and take those as the basis for his grammar. Naturally, the forms that he describes may include some that he has never heard, or heard only under conditions of substantial interference.

This is what dialectologists do. I do not know if it is always what they say they do. But in Scotland, for example, the problem has long been clear.

§78. The preceding section may seem a digression. Our problem is to account for variation, not to find means by which we avoid doing so.

But our generativist may seize on the notion of interference. The standard language interferes, it is said, with the dialect; but, naturally, the effect is greater for some speakers than for others. Speaker A will mostly talk the dialect; however, he sometimes uses standard words instead, sometimes his vowels are more like standard vowels, and so on. Here we have an aged shepherd, our dialectologist's best subject. Then there is the landowner's factor B. He mostly talks the regional standard; however, in speaking to A he sometimes uses words in the dialect, his vowels are often nearer to A's than to the standard, and so on. So there is variation, in the speech both of the individual and of the community at large.

Why should the interference take place?

"Again, because both speakers know both forms of speech. Both are bilingual."

§79. For the descriptive linguist this proposal is quite attractive. Historically there may be a superstratum and a substratum: the dialect developed in virtual isolation; then the standard came in with improved communication. Substratum dialects are here no more than a special case of substratum languages. Welsh was spoken in isolation, but has suffered progressive interference from English. If it helps to say so, then a shepherd in Westmorland is bilingual in qualitatively the same sense as a shepherd in Snowdonia.

Suppose we want to describe the actual speech of the locality. First, we could write a dialect grammar on the lines of §77; this is merely another form of what Lyons calls standardisation (§§54, 63). Then we write a grammar of the standard; this may involve a similar idealisation. Next we compare one system with the other, and note possible points of interference. Our data are then explained by reference to both.

For a Scottish illustration see, for instance, Wölck's phonology of the Buchan district of Aberdeenshire [42]. A more striking study is that of Bickerton on Guyanan Creole [43]; here there are three systems – a so-called 'basilect', 'mesolect' and 'acrolect'.

§80. In the last section we are still concerned with problems of description. I should stress that Bickerton himself repudiates hypotheses of multilingualism.

"But surely it does give us insights into the speaker's competence. Thus for your simplest case a natural account would be like this.

"First, we can say that every speaker has internalised the rules of the dialect; let us show this with a solid circle representing the language so specified.

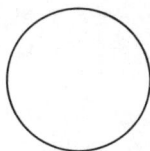

Secondly, he has internalised the rules of the standard; let us show this with another solid circle.

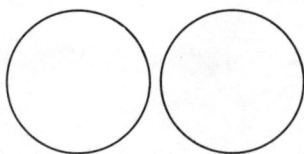

Naturally, this is what we would also envisage for bilingual speakers in Wales.

"But then these sets of rules will clash at various points. Let us therefore imagine certain general 'rules of interaction' – part, perhaps, of Chomsky's general human faculty of language. These would map the languages together; they would relate possible dialect sentences to possible standard sentences. They would also define a range of intermediate sentences: dialect sentences with just one standard feature substituted, standard sentences with just one dialect feature, and so on. The possible sentences as a whole could thus be represented by a larger oval

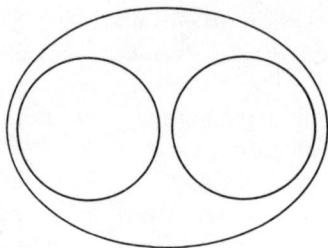

properly including both the pure dialect and the pure standard. It is this larger set that is instanced in our data."

§81. Would this explain the facts? No, as it stands it obviously would not. In particular, it does not explain the differences between speakers.

Have A and B internalised identical sets of rules – both the same dialect grammar and the same standard grammar? On the proposal as it appears, yes. But A, we supposed, was much more of a dialect speaker and B much more of a standard speaker. Why so?

"Well, the difference lies not in their competence but in their use of it. They know both languages; but the shepherd naturally tends to use his dialect competence more often than his standard competence, and the factor *vice versa*."

This will reduce to a variant of Labov's proposal, and is open to similar objections (§§65–75).

§82. "Then perhaps their grammars are different. The shepherd's dialect rules are for a purer dialect than the factor's, and the factor's standard rules for a purer standard than the shepherd's."

But would that account for all our facts? Take the situation in Jamaica, for instance. Here there is a range – some writers would say a continuum – between the Creole and the standard. But according to reports, an individual's speech is not restricted to one segment of it. Sometimes an educated speaker utters forms in pure Creole: say, a word with the extreme Creole vowel sound. An uneducated speaker sometimes utters purely standard forms. Why so, if their grammars do not include them?

"Well, why not? Surely it is natural that, in performance, they should sometimes overshoot their competence."

But why in that specific way? We are supposing that each speaker knows two separate languages, one higher and one lower on the range for the community. It is the pull between these that establishes his usual performance. But he has not internalised the whole range: A's standard grammar is not the same as B's, nor B's dialect grammar the same as A's. So, if A speaks B's standard, it is by overshooting; likewise if B speaks A's dialect. How do they get it right? Why should one's overshot speech be correct for the other's usual speech?

Plainly each must know the rest of the range too. But they would have to know it in a different sort of way. What would we mean by these two different sorts of knowledge?

§83. Such speakers seem to have a knowledge of the whole range, plus a weighting of this knowledge which would vary from one individual to another. Of course, that was precisely the point of Labov's proposal (§67). But our colleague might now suggest another mechanism.

"Let us suppose, first of all, that every speaker has what we may call his *own language* – one language, that is, on which his speech is centred. This we can again represent with a solid circle.

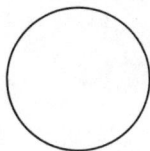

If all speakers had the same own language, that alone (barring performance factors) would determine how they spoke. But this is an ideal, as Chomsky himself recognises. A much-cited passage at the beginning of *Aspects* ([7], p. 3) makes this perfectly clear.

"Then what happens in a non-homogeneous community? Our speaker B will have an own language tending (let us say) towards the standard. However, he often talks to A, whose speech is heavily dialectal, and in this way he will form a *conception* (maybe accurate, maybe inaccurate) of what A's language is like. Let us therefore add a separate broken circle

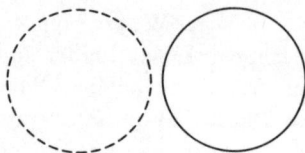

representing the set of sentences specified by his conception of A's rules. He will also talk to C, whose speech (let us say) is intermediate between the two; in this way he will form a conception of a further language which, as shown,

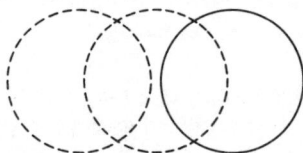

might overlap the two preceding. Then he will also talk to D, whose speech is even less dialectal than his own; he will thus form a conception of D's language too.

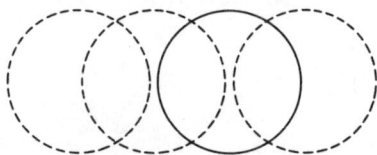

More generally, we can say that he forms conceptions of 'the language of people like A', 'the language of people like C', 'the language of people like D', and so on. Finally, there will be other people who, he conceives, have a language identical to his own.

"Now what happens in actual speech situations? Let us suppose that B is talking to E, whose language he conceives as identical to his own. Naturally he will try to speak according to the rules of the own language that he has internalised. But there will be interference from his conceptions of other people's languages; sometimes he will produce forms which are more like C's or D's. His *possible sentences* (in the sense of §80) may accordingly be represented by a slightly larger oval properly including those of his own language as such.

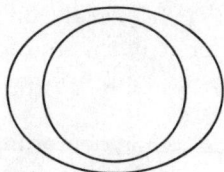

"Then let us suppose that he is talking to A. Naturally he will adapt his speech in accordance with his conception of A's language. But against this there will be interference from at least the rules of his own language: sometimes he will utter his own forms, sometimes his conception of A's forms, more often something in between. So, his possible sentences may be represented by a larger oval which in this case will obviously include both.

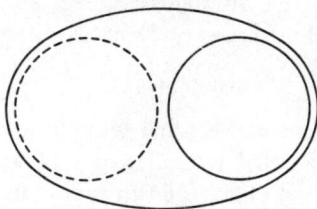

In general, there will be similar interference whenever he is talking to someone like A, someone like C, someone like D, and so on.

"To sum up, his range of possible sentences may be represented by a series of larger ovals, one for every case of interference.

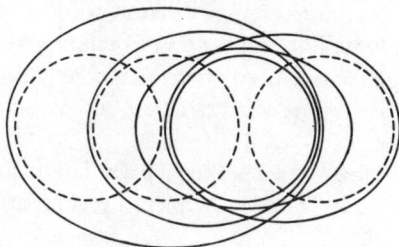

Between them they cover the whole range in the community; that is the answer to the Jamaican problem (§82). But they each include the speaker's own language; that is why the shepherd's speech is different from the factor's (§81). Finally, different ranges are selected when the speaker is talking to different people; that is the answer to our original problem of the bank manager's secretary (§62)."

§84. Here we have a full elaboration of the proposal first mooted apropos of semi-productivity (§27). If the speaker has such a competence, I cannot show that it would not account for his performance. The problem, rather, is how he comes to acquire it.

How, for example, does B acquire his conception of the language of people like A?

"Well, he listens to a number of people like A and he constructs a set of rules which accounts for their speech."

Then how does he acquire his own language? Obviously, he listens to a number of people and constructs a set of rules which accounts for their speech. So, all his languages (solid circle and dotted circles) are acquired in that way. What is so special about the one which we have called 'his own language'?

§85. There are certain answers that will obviously not do.

One is to suppose that it is a matter of active versus passive competence. This might have been an answer in the case of *messaged that* and so forth (see again §§26–7). Thus the speaker might not have *messaged that* in his own language (active competence), and so does not utter it; but it is in his conception of other people's languages (passive competence), and so might be accepted if presented to him. But now it is all a matter of active competence.

Nor can we account for it in terms of native versus foreign languages. For B is not conscious that at some stage he is learning to talk like A. He will not report that in talking to A he is speaking another language. It is all 'his own language' so far as he is concerned.

So what establishes the solid circle in our diagram?

§86. "Well, obviously, a speaker's own language is the one he acquires in childhood. The rest he picks up later, after his childhood learning is complete."

But children are not kept in purdah until their 'own grammar' is completed. What is envisaged – that they listen to homogeneous speech until they are such and such an age? And then they are let loose into the world to listen to other people's speech? But the parents themselves may not speak in precisely the same way. Then the child plays with the neighbours' children, he is taken out shopping, he has tea with his aunt, and so on.

"Yes, but we do not have to assume that the language formed in childhood will be learned in the same way as the conceptions of languages formed later.

"Chomsky has proposed that each child has a special language acquisition device (LAD). This has the ability to ignore hesitations, slips in performance, and so on. But it could also have a capacity for standardisation (§63). Suppose it takes one speaker as the norm: all else being equal, the child's mother. Perhaps her speech varies; then certain variants are selected, and the others treated as performance errors. The speech of other individuals (father, aunts, and so on) may show other variants; these too will be converted into standardised forms. The input to the LAD is thus made homogeneous; it is from this homogenised corpus that a grammar for the child's own language is constructed.

"Then, when its task is done, the LAD will cease to operate. The speaker's mind will become open to other speakers' variants. Conceptions of their languages will then be formed by other processes.

"Surely this hypothesis protects my model from your line of criticism."

§87. Indeed it is very difficult to argue with a *deus ex machina*. But there are problems, still, when a person's language subsequently changes.

Let us imagine the following speaker. He was born on a farm near Totnes, and as a boy he mainly spoke the local dialect. For example, he tended to use West Country pronouns (*Don' 'ee touch 'un!*) rather than the standard system. He joined the army when he was 17, later marrying a girl from the London area. In the end he rose to regimental sergeant major, and is now retired and living in Chelsea Hospital. Throughout his career his speech has been increasingly modified. For example, as a non-commissioned officer he regularly used the standard pronouns (*Don't you touch it!*), even in addressing recruits from his own district. In general his speech has developed characteristics similar to that of other long-serving warrant officers.

Now, how would we account for this development?

§88. Has his own language remained the same since boyhood?

According to the hypothesis (§86) the answer must be yes. One's own language is the one constructed by the special LAD. By the time the speaker was 10 (shall we say?) the LAD had ceased to be effective. Any language learned later can only be a conception of another's language.

But then we cannot explain his speech in later life. Say he started to learn German in his fifties, perhaps on a long tour after Hitler's war. Naturally, there was interference from his English; but what English? His original Devonshire dialect? Or mainly that, even? I do not know the facts of such cases, but it seems implausible. After this tour he will have had home leave and gone back to his birth-place. Will he immediately have reverted to his boyhood speech? That is what ought to have happened, according to the hypothesis of §83. But in fact it would not have happened, would it?

How can we say his language does not shift, when his speech does?

§89. "Very well, let us suppose that it does shift. At the beginning, he will have had his 'own dialect'; this we can represent as before.

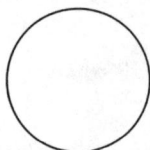

At some later stage he forms his 'conception of a warrant officer's language'; nevertheless the dialect, for the moment, remains his own language.

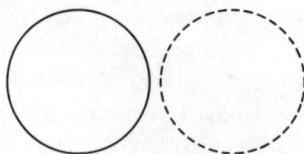

Then, later still, the relationship is reversed. The warrant officer's language becomes his own language,

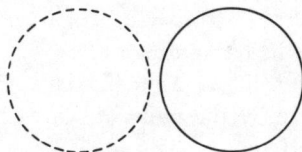

the dialect then remaining merely as a conception of another's language. At each stage the effects of interference follow as before."

In brief, at some point there is a switch of languages. Before this the dialect interferes with his ability to speak like a warrant officer. After it his warrant officer's language interferes with his ability to speak the dialect.

§90. But how did this come about? First, why did this speaker switch languages when many others do not?

"Well, this has to be explained by practice and motivation. In the army he spoke less and less with other speakers of his dialect; at the same time he spoke more and more with the non-commissioned officers of his regiment. So, he had far more practice in speaking like a non-commissioned officer than, shall we say, our shepherd ever had in speaking like the factor. There were also obvious motives: a warrant officer's speech would help to set him in the regimental hierarchy. The shepherd had less motive for talking differently."

Indeed so. But as with Labov's proposal (§§69, 73-4), we are beginning to suffer from an excess of hypotheses. Some speakers, we say, have an own language which is so by virtue of the special LAD. Others have an own language which is so by virtue of practice and motivation. Why do we need both types of explanation? Why not say of any speaker that his own language is the one which he has the greatest motive to speak and in which he has had the greatest practice?

§91. And how did he acquire his non-commissioned officer's language to begin with? That is, how did he arrive at the second stage of §89?

"Well, obviously, he put together a certain set of rules. In part these are the same rules as his dialect, in part new rules are added, in part the rules may be re-ordered. Together they form an additional grammar that he has internalised."

Then at what point did he internalise it?

"Well, presumably by the point at which his speech begins to exhibit signs of interference."

So, at first he uses nothing but the dialect forms. (Let us allow an advantage in our adversary's favour.) Then, sporadically, his speech shows modifications. As soon as this happens we can say: 'Now he has internalised the rules of what will later be his own language.'

But this is astonishing – that he should have learned a language ('put together a certain set of rules') before it has the slightest effect on his speech. Not even the child's LAD is supposed to be able to do that.

§92. What would be a more likely answer? In some way, it seems, the speaker must acquire his non-commissioned officer's language (learn to speak like a non-commissioned officer) gradually.

Let us reflect on the facts. He joins his regiment; at first he speaks only his dialect. But this is not the speech he always hears around him: in particular, not that of the corporal and other soldiers with longer service. So, gradually, he begins to adapt to his surroundings. He begins to speak a little like the corporal, just as he begins to carry himself a little like the corporal, and so on. Naturally, the first effects are slight and sporadic; he still speaks mainly as he did before he enlisted. But gradually, again, he gets more practice. More and more, his tendency to speak the dialect is overcome; more and more, he begins to utter his superiors' forms correctly. As time passes he gets his first stripe, then his second and third. He will begin to have conversations with the company sergeant major, with his platoon commander, and so on. His tendency to speak like a non-commissioned officer grows even stronger.

If a man's speech changes gradually how can it be governed by rules that change all of a sudden?

§93. "Then let us posit some form of gradual learning. But in the end he still constructs the grammar of his non-commissioned officer's language."

What do we gain by saying so?

At some point in his life our speaker does not have the grammar of this language. The process of constructing its rules is not complete. Nevertheless he sometimes uses non-commissioned officers' forms. Why? Since he has not internalised their grammar we are forced to posit some other factor (let us call it factor X) that is responsible.

Then at a later point he does have the grammar. That can provide an explanation from then on. But it is not needed. If factor X was sufficient before, it is sufficient still.

And at what point will the grammar have taken over? It seems a wholly arbitrary decision. What evidence could bear on it?

§94. "Nevertheless he *must* have internalised it. For remember, the language which it generates is the one which we are calling his own language later."

But it is not clear why *that* part of the hypothesis is needed. For the same gradual process will continue. Our sergeant is promoted to company sergeant major and then to regimental sergeant major; with still more practice his army speech gets better and better. By the end he is in no sense a speaker of the Devonshire dialect.

"At some point, that is, the rules of the army language came to dominate his competence."

But at exactly what point? Again it would be an arbitrary decision. So why say it happens? Might not factor X again provide sufficient explanation?

§95. "Well, he constructed the grammar of one language in his childhood; that was his original linguistic competence. We agree that his speech has changed. That is, he no longer performs entirely in accordance with his original rules. That means he must have developed a new competence – a new set of rules – in their place."

Now my colleague is directly begging the question. I attack the view that children construct grammars; it is defended by the suggestion that adults can construct additional grammars. I attack this, and it is defended on the grounds that grammars *are* constructed by children.

It was perhaps unfair to put these words into my colleague's mouth. For he will see the way my argument is going. The child is born and gradually again, adapts himself to his surroundings. Gradually he comes to speak like his parents, just as he comes to hold a knife and fork like his parents, and so on. Of course, the results are quicker and more spectacular. The child has not learned to speak before; there are no earlier forms of speech to offer resistance. But still the process is gradual. The child begins to speak before we have the slightest grounds to postulate a grammar.

For this last point may I refer to my review of Brown's book in the *Journal of Linguistics* [44, 25]? But we need not go into the details of children's language. At some point we are forced to postulate a learning process other than the construction of grammars – what we called factor X (§93). Why should it not operate from the beginning?

§96. How would my friend react in conclusion? I think he would again start on his spiel about scientific hypotheses (compare §56).

"Look, we are putting forward a scientific theory. We postulate that the child constructs a grammar; in connection with this we postulate a certain sort of learning process. If the speech community were homogeneous that would be all.

"But it is not all. The speaker, we postulate, can form a conception of another speaker's language. This too must be represented by a set of generative rules; he does not simply imitate specific forms. In connection with this we may postulate a different sort of learning process.

"Some speakers forms few such conceptions, and the effect on their speech is weak. Others form many such conceptions, and their effect is strong. For others, again, one such conception may eventually come to dominate their earlier grammar.

"There, that is our theory. Have you produced one shred of real empirical evidence against it?"

§97. Have you any real evidence against alternative theories? But that would be a cheap answer. For this argument is not of the sort that our friend wants it to be.

Let us imagine a man who is trying to draw a circle with a ruler. 'Look, I have split it into fifteen lines and already it is getting very like it.'

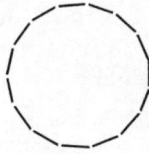

But that, we will tell him, is not the way to draw a circle. Here, let us give you a pair of compasses; then you can draw it easily.

'But look, this is my empirical hypothesis. Every extra line I draw confirms it. What counter-evidence have you that would falsify it?'

Neither this man, nor my generativist, would be arguing reasonably.

§98. Let us remind ourselves of the sort of explanations we would be asked to accept.

At some point our RSM has finished internalising his army language. So, six months beforehand, he is still at the stage of learning it gradually. A year later, he is speaking according to its rules – except that his own dialect rules keep interfering. But is there any qualitative change in his behaviour? No, none whatever.

At a later point this army language becomes his own language. So, six months beforehand, he is speaking according to his conception of his comrades' language; only, by gradual processes, the interference from his dialect is substantially overcome. A year later, he is speaking in accordance with what is now his own language; only, of course, there is some interference from his conception of the dialect. Again, is there any qualitative change in his behaviour? No, none whatever.

Have I evidence that these are wrong explanations? Of course, we have oversimplified the whole affair. Our speaker will use one sort of speech on the parade ground, another in the sergeants' mess. There are many other factors pulling one way or another: for example, his regiment is stationed for a while in his home county. Then we have said nothing about his wife's speech, about his children's, and so on. But would the theory be vulnerable to such complications? No, we would just be offered more of the same sort of explanation. For example, at some point he has internalised the rules of a parade-ground language.

The real objection is like our objection to the man with the ruler.

Why ever should we want to explain things in this way? A man's speech varies continuously – to and fro, upwards and downwards – throughout his life. Why should we try and reduce this to the interaction of a series of discrete languages?

There seems no reason at all, except that languages of this sort are what are characterised by generative grammars. How else could our generativist maintain that he is using the right instrument?

MEANING

§99. The heading may seem odd at this stage; surely we have been talking about meaning ever since we discussed Hockett's argument. Of course we have. Indeed, that is the trouble with so many theories of meaning: that they say nothing about dialect variation, nothing about semi-productive processes, and so on. As accounts of human communication they do not come under starter's orders.

However, there are other problems which semanticists have typically thought of as their own. What do we learn from them?

The best known are those of word meaning (§§103 and following). These teach us the same lesson that we learned from our discussion of semi-productivity (§§24–35): that the lexicon is of its nature ill defined. But problems of sentence meaning have again come to the fore (§§119 and following). The lesson they teach is the one we began to inculcate in §§39 and following: that there is no line dividing what belongs and what does not belong to the language system.

§100. Chomsky's theory of the sentence is explained with sufficient clarity.

According to him a sentence is a mental object; in characterising such objects we are characterising the speaker's competence, not his performance. (This our objector has already explained, in §21.) Each sentence has both a form and a meaning: so, its description must include a *semantic representation* (SR), just as it includes a *phonetic representation* (PR). Both SR and PR are again mental objects; both are specified by rule as part of a total structural description. Both too are represented in terms independent of the particular language; there must be a universal set of categories by which we represent meanings (SRs), just as there is another by which we represent phonetic signals (PRs). Any particular grammar maps particular SRs on to particular PRs in an unambiguous way.

Chomsky has often said that we know little about semantic representation. (A more damaging admission will be cited later, in §132.) But his programmatic statements are clear. 'It is quite obvious', he writes, 'that sentences have an intrinsic meaning determined by linguistic rule and that a person with command of a language has in some way internalized the system of rules that determine both the phonetic shape of the sentence and its intrinsic semantic content' (appendix to Lenneberg [45], p. 397). 'It seems clear that we must regard linguistic competence – knowledge of a language – as . . . a system constituted by rules that interact to determine the form and intrinsic meaning of a potentially infinite number of sentences' (*Language and Mind* [46], p. 71). To reject that is to reject the essence of his theory of language.

§101. A generativist's view of sentence meaning immediately limits his view of word meaning. SRs have a formal characterisation; therefore so must their constituents.

Its specification might take various forms. Some scholars envisage a dictionary, where each word has a set of semantic features. (So *kill* has one while *die* has another; but between them certain features are in common, as between either and the sets assigned to *murder*, *decease*, and so on.) For others there is no dictionary, but certain parts of SRs form the input to successive rules of lexicalisation. (So *kill* derives from one structure and *die* from another, but in part they are identical.) Other scholars propose both.

Such differences do not concern us, any more than deep structure, generative phonology, and so on (§2). All that is crucial is that words too are in some way subject to rule.

Word Meaning

§102. What is the basis for Chomskyan theories of word meaning? Essentially, that each word has a *definition*. This is known to the speaker, it is said, as part of his linguistic competence.

In that light a sentence is described as deviant or non-deviant, contradictory or non-contradictory, and so on. There is a contradiction (it might be said) in *I killed John but he didn't die*; that would be explained by the definitions assignable to *kill* and *die*. *The stillness killed the tomatoes* might be treated as a deviant sentence. Or perhaps it might not. That would reflect a difference in the definitions of *kill* or *stillness*.

All this is made clear in the leading article by Katz and Fodor [47]. A definition might be given in different ways, as we have just remarked (§101). But it must be given precisely, like the rules of syntax or phonology. If not, the speaker's judgements of contradiction, deviance, and so on are not explicated.

§103. But this project was without hope. For it ascribes to the speaker's knowledge things that we, as scholars, know from long experience we cannot know.

Most of the reasons are in any decently old-fashioned textbook. For the rest we must refer specifically to Wittgenstein's analysis of *game* ([34], §§66–71); also to Bolinger's important critique of Katz and Fodor [48]. The point is echoed by at least one generative semanticist: Lakoff, in a paper on 'fuzzy concepts' to the Chicago Linguistic Society [49].

Let us rehearse the lesson with just four or five examples.

§104. An obvious problem is the boundary of homonymy and polysemy.

The speaker says that he will 'strike a match'; also that 'the match was won' by so and so. Has he internalised two different words or only one? We will doubtless judge that there are two words, *match*$_1$ and *match*$_2$. Their identity of form has no semantic motivation.

He hopes that 'the weather will be fair'; he also says that his wife has 'fair hair'. Here we might judge that there is one word, *fair*, which has been used in two different senses. Or perhaps we might not. It depends on whether we see a connection between them.

But when is there a connection and when not a connection? A 'truss' may be something that is worn to retain a hernia. Another sort of truss (according to my dictionary) is used to secure a yardarm to a mast. Another is the truss of a triangular roof, or another bracing member of that kind. And then one also talks of a truss of tomatoes. Is there a connection between the first two? Well, they are both

intended to tie or hold something in place. Then the first three?
Well, the truss in a building is something which ties the structure
together. But is it 'tying' of a similar enough sort? And what of the
last? Does the speaker think of the tomatoes as some sort of bundle?

A dictionary must give one entry or two. But dictionaries decide
by the history, or follow others that do so. Between the *OED* and
the speaker there is again no comparison (§6).

§105. "But does it matter which the child decides? All we are
saying is that some decision is made. Some set of lexical entries,
or their equivalent, is internalised."

Then let us take just one word, and in just one sense. Still it may
have no precise definition.

In his book on translation Mounin compares a classification of
buildings to a botanical classification ([50]), p. 88). For example, we
count the number of storeys: if there are 'more than fifteen' it is a
skyscraper (*gratte-ciel*), but if there are less than 'ten or fifteen' it is
not. But this vagueness is precisely to the point. Let us think of a
building with just fourteen storeys: is it a skyscraper or not? Of
course a skyscraper is one sort of tall building. But it is vain to try
and say exactly how tall.

Perhaps it is time we used some jargon. We are supposed to
determine the 'extension' of such words. So we might ask: 'What
are the conditions under which *That is a skyscraper* would express a
true proposition?' But ordinary words tend not to have exact
extensions or intensions.

§106. We can easily elaborate the example. Let us imagine that this
building has been put up in the nearest village street.

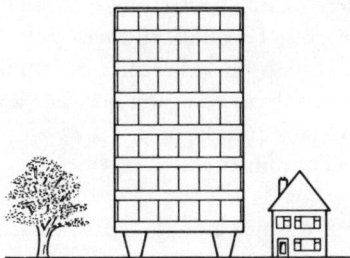

'Heavens!', we say, 'What *do* they want with that sort of sky-scraper?' Suppose someone objected. 'But is it a skycraper? Look, it is only seven storeys high. If you put it down in Manhattan you would hardly notice it was there.' – Well, so what? The village is not Manhattan, and there the description fits.

"Ah! But now you are talking about the emotive use of language. A pigsty, for example, is a place where one keeps pigs. But I might say of the Bloggins's that 'they live in a pigsty out in Oxfordshire'. This is to use *pigsty* in a further figurative sense. Or maybe it is to coin a metaphor for the occasion. Likewise there is something figurative about this use of *skyscraper*."

Perhaps so. But where does the basic use end and the figurative use begin? And is the latter indeed part of the language – so part of the speaker's competence – or is it indeed coined in performance?

These too are questions which we know we cannot always answer.

§107. A dictionary defines words by other words. The imprecision of the noun *skyscraper* can thus be reflected in the imprecision of the adjectives *tall* or *high* or *narrow*. But this technique can fail.

What, for example, is a 'pin'? According to the *Oxford English Dictionary*:

A small piece of wood, metal, or other solid substance, of cylindrical or similar shape, often tapering or pointed, used for some one of various purposes, as to fasten or hold together parts of a structure, to hang something upon, to stop up a hole, or as a part of a mechanism to convey or check motion; a peg, a bolt.

Well, what do we call the tapering spike of metal which we use to fasten carpets to the floor? Is that a pin? No, it is a tack. What does one call the cylinders of metal that plugged into holes in switchboards? Were those pins? I would call them jacks.

So what *are* the defining characteristics of a pin? It is a forlorn question. For there is more in common between a tack and a drawing pin, or between a jack and the pins of a 13-amp plug, than there is between the different pins themselves.

§108. "Then perhaps it is not a single word. Perhaps it is a series of homonyms."

But for anything we do call a pin we can find others that are somewhat like it. The pin of an electric plug has something in common with the pin in golf, and both, perhaps, have something in common with the safety pin of a grenade. They are all pins which fit into their respective holes. But then the safety pin has much in common with thole-pins or other pins that hold an assembly together; this introduces the element of 'fastening'. Golf pins also mark a position on the ground; one sticks little pins into maps for the same purpose. But we can also mark the map with ribbons, and the pins we use for that can also be used to pin papers to a board; thus we arrive at fastening by a different route. But then we can use another pointed pin to pin papers or cloth together; this leads to a dress-maker's safety pin and, in another direction, to a hat pin and a tie pin.

In short, we have a series of what Wittgenstein called family resemblances.

§109. "Then perhaps it is one word, but with several different senses. We agree that some pins are characterised by pointedness; so, if a woman is said to have 'pricked her finger with a pin', the hearer is not likely to take it as a golf pin. That, then, is a feature marking one group of senses; it is shared by *needle* and by certain other items in our lexicon. Then there are other features of fastening, and so on. Their intersections will define our individual sub-entries."

The snag is in the words 'and so on'. For, as Bolinger has shown, there is no limit to the marking features we might posit.

They chopped up the wire for firewood – there is something anomalous about this. Doubtless we assign *wire* the semantic marker [+ metal]. *They chopped up the pins for firewood* – the hearer is likely to take it that they were not dress-making pins. So does *pin* have senses which are [+metal], opposed to others which are [+wooden]? Golf pins might be wood or might not. So would there be different senses, [+ golf, + wooden, . . .] and [+ golf, − wooden, . . .]?

§110. Nor is it clear, again, precisely what the word *pin* can be used of.

Take the compounds *tie pin*, *drawing pin*, and so on. These two are among its hyponyms: for instance, I can say *He wore a red tie with a diamond-studded pin*. But what of *hairpin* or *panel pin*? Suppose that someone is by me ready to hand me panel pins: would I ask him *Now could I have the pins?* or *Now could I have the nails?* I would not swear to my usage.

I lock my bicycle with a padlock like this.

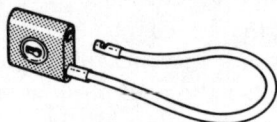

As you see, there is a cable with a whatsit on the end which locks into a hole in the usual way. Well, what does one call such a 'whatsit'? Say one is trying to show a child how it works: *Look, one pushes the pin into the hole and*... Is that a new use of *pin*? Or a deviant use? Or just a normal use? I do not know how one could be expected to answer.

§111. The arguments may be compared to arguments about the treatment of morphemes.

A case has various uses, divided and exemplified in grammars. Are these effective homonyms, each having its own rule? (That is the tendency in generative treatments.)

But no. The uses are connected, like those of *pin* (§108). Nor is their number determinate (as for *pin* in §§109–10). Then should we seek some general meaning, however empty it may be? (That was the line of Jakobson and others.)

Again no. Just as there are family resemblances, so there are no more than family resemblances.

Compare Bazell's classic remarks on 'correspondence fallacies' [51]. Whichever way we jump, it is at root the same error.

§112. Indeed it is hard for me to say anything original. Nor was it easy for the generativists themselves.

I have already referred to Mounin on translation [50], from the same year as Katz and Fodor's big splash. This also surveys earlier work in French lexicology. For a closer parallel see the monograph by Greimas [52], still in the mid-sixties. Long before, a theory of features or figurae was put forward by Hjelmslev. In the United

States, we may compare the stratificationalist revival of the sememe.
Let there be no silly talk of generative grammar versus structuralism (§14).

§113. "Then do you want to condemn all schools at once?"
Indeed I do not wish to condemn. For even shaky ideas can have
their uses.

Many scholars have adopted a triangular model of meaning –
words related to objects *via* concepts. The speaker has in his mind a
concept 'pin', and certain objects are conceived as corresponding to
it. The concept is in turn related to the word *pin*. So, by virtue of
these correspondences he says *Those are pins*.

If taken that way then of course it will not do. Yet the model
itself is useful. Suppose we are talking about semantic fields; that of
'love and courtship' might be a typical example. We will look at
language A to see how its vocabulary is structured. Maybe we will
compare it with another language B, or with A itself at earlier
periods. We will talk of ways in which the field is split up: doubtless
too of finer sub-fields covering 'dating', 'chaperones', or what not.
Perhaps A has a single term for 'sexual play' in general, while B has
a series of terms for socially recognised gradations. 'Love and courtship', 'dating', 'sexual play' – all these are concepts which are set up
in the analysis of either system. They are the necessary framework
for comparison.

Why should the objections worry us? It is not a philosophical
problem we are attacking. And what is the alternative? Only to
engage in quite unnecessary circumlocution. By talking of concepts
we can set aside irrelevant issues.

But practical models tend to give themselves airs. The triangle is
elaborated into a complex system: see, for example, the latter part
of Baldinger's *Semantic Theory* [53]. One talks of fields and concepts
which exist in isolation from particular languages: compare 'a
language-independent alphabet of semantic representation'. The
concepts are foisted on to the speaker's 'consciousness'. Then we
must cry halt.

§114. A dictionary is another commonsense project. Naturally it
has its problems: for example, in establishing sets and hierarchies

of senses. A feature analysis will often help to solve such difficulties. Of the French work which I mentioned, some springs directly from the concerns of practical lexicographers. In that case, our evaluation would be different.

What we must condemn is the reification – the systematic ambiguity (§4) by which the meaning of a word is something at once specified by the linguist and internalised by the speaker.

§115. How does our generativist envisage semantic change? In the normal account the imprecision of words is a central factor.

We have already spoken of lexical creativity (§35). At times a new form is established: for instance, when a certain gadget was called a 'toaster'. At other times a sense is extended: for instance, when the screen of a television set was called a 'screen'. In neither case are speakers governed by rules; in neither do they break rules.

It is here that Hockett's misgivings (§20) are most clearly justified. In natural languages 'no word is ever limited to its enumerable senses'; it always 'carries within it' the qualification of 'something like'. (I am citing Bolinger [48], p. 567.) If we ignore this we indeed ignore the property which is most important (Hockett [15], loc. cit.). For a language without it would be most unnatural; how could it respond to speakers' needs?

§116. "Yes, we know all that. But let us look more closely at your example.

"At one stage, *screen* was used of firescreens, cinema screens, and so on. Then some speakers started to use it of the screens of cathode ray tubes; from them the new application spread. Now consider a speaker A, who meets it for the first time: suppose someone explains *And then you see a picture on the glass screen*. A's lexicon will lack this sense; therefore, for him, the sentence must be deviant. He may understand it: there is only one screen-like thing it could refer to. But he might have difficulty. (*Sorry, what screen are you talking about?*)

"Later, A himself begins to use *screen* in the same way. At that point there are two possibilities. At first the sense may still be missing from his competence; strictly speaking, his use is deviant. He might even excuse himself. (*Well, that's what people call it.*) Or perhaps he may already have internalised it. Sooner or later he will certainly do so.

"In our account there has indeed been first a rule break, then a rule change. Bolinger's 'something like' means simply that a similar use can be intelligible in performance."

But such accounts can only be given in the light of subsequent analysis. Take the man who spoke to A about 'the glass screen'. Perhaps he had not called it that before; but he wanted a word and found one. Did this at once enlarge his competence?

"Not necessarily. Perhaps it was deviant by his rules too."

But why are those the only alternatives?

"Well surely, we agree that we are dealing with a new sense. So, either he has or he has not internalised it."

Indeed you see it as a new sense, now it is established. But that has no bearing on its first use, or its first use by that speaker. Suppose that *screen* did apply to cinema screens; so, he used it of another 'whatsit' which shows moving images. Why should this be either a new sense or a deviance from the old one?

§117. Let us add one hoary illustration. We agree that the word *pen* derives from an ancient word for 'feather'; on the molar level this is a classic shift of meaning. Then must we speak of sudden changes in each individual's competence – when quills were first adapted to writing, then again when metal nibs were substituted? Has my own grammar changed when I applied the same word to ballpoints?

If we work such cases through we will be in more knots than we ever were with our sergeant major (§§87–98).

§118. Chomsky himself has said little about word meaning; I am forced to rely on his endorsement of Katz and Fodor. But their article [47] is fifteen years old. I know that Fodor no longer supports it. Are we pushing against a door that is already open?

Alas, no. I mentioned an article by Lakoff [49]. It is combated in a recent study by Katz and Bever [54], where they insist that fuzziness is in performance only.

Sentence Meaning

§119. When we turn to sentence meaning we are faced with serious problems in interpreting the literature. We have Chomsky's programmatic statements (§100); but he has tended not to discuss the type of example which seems crucial. His disciples have provided illustrations galore. But many have come to reject his programme.

We must therefore begin by considering the issues more widely.

§120. Traditionally, a sentence is the expression of a thought – the 'complete thought' of one familiar class of definitions. Unfortunately, the tradition seems not to be dead.

According to Chafe,

> In its broadest outline, language involves the following process. A configuration of concepts arises within the nervous system of a human being [! P.H.M.] who, for some reason, often but not necessarily associated with purposeful communication, is led to convert these concepts into sound . . . (*Meaning and the Structure of Language* [55], p. 17)

So, there are possible 'configurations of concepts' (again, let us call them SRs), there are possible sound configurations (PRs), and there is a relation between them which we might call the relation of 'potential exteriorisation'. The SR 'It is raining' then arises in the speaker's nervous system – I am trying to illustrate with Chafe's example (p. 18) – and may be exteriorised by the PR *It is raining*. Accordingly the speaker may say *It is raining*. In writing the grammar of a language we are describing this relation between SRs and PRs.

What now would be the difference between sentence meaning and utterance meaning? Apparently it would be a difference between types and tokens. I say *It is raining* at nine o'clock some morning: my utterance is a token of the sentence-type *It is raining*. I say it because I have the thought 'It is raining': this is likewise a token of the thought-type 'It is raining'.

§121. Chafe is not a spokesman for the generative school. Nor is this Chomsky's theory (§100). But in the later sixties other scholars began to talk the same way. In this lies the origin of the movement inappropriately known as 'generative semantics'.

My clearest reference is to an introductory book by Langacker [56], published in 1968. Langacker talks of a 'conceptual structure' as 'the thought that a speaker wants to express' (p. 86); it is represented in the grammar by the input to the transformational component. This view he relates to those which Lakoff and others were developing.

Other writers are less lucid. But Ross on declaratives [57] speaks at one point of a 'pragmatic analysis'. This 'claims that certain elements are present in the context of a speech act, and that syntactic processes can refer to such elements' (p. 254). So, the context would provide an '*I*' (Ross's italic) which is 'in the air' (Ross's inverted commas); a transformation can then take this as, for instance, the antecedent of a reflexive (*As for myself*, . . .). The analysis provides an alternative to underlying *I say* . . .

In what theory would that make sense? Not in that of Chomsky's *Aspects* [7], since the *I* is not part of a deep structure. Nor in any theory in which SRs are 'intrinsic meanings' (§100); for they are independent of 'the context of a speech act'. Therefore not in the ostensible theory of generative semantics (as Chomsky criticised it in contemporary papers [6]); for that merely eliminated the syntactic base component. But it does make sense – in so far as sense is possible – within the Chafe-like theory I have outlined. The speaker has a thought, in the context of utterance, and on that the grammatical processes operate.

In reviewing this passage I was led to wonder [58] if the generative theory of the sentence might be on its way out. A year or two later and I would have been more certain.

§122. Let us now consider some of the obvious properties of utterance meaning.

Take the following conversation:

A. I did go through Exeter last week.
B. Oh. Did you have time for the cathedral?
A. Yes. But I'm sorry, I don't think the east window is *quite* so good.
B. Well, you must forgive my local patriotism.
A. But why didn't you tell me about the vault?

Our speakers have understood each other perfectly. A is a Yorkshireman, B a Devonian. When they last met A had been extolling the glass in York Minster (which B had at some time visited). B knew that A might be going down to Devon; why didn't he look at the cathedral there? The east window, B said, is as good as anything York has got. But, of course, the beauty of Exeter is in its whole interior, especially in the vaulting of the nave and choir. The great window, though fine, is not so remarkable as the Five Sisters. So, when they meet again . . .

Some of this can be gathered from the conversation itself. A says he 'did go' through Exeter; this presupposes that there was a possibility of his going, but that it was in doubt. He does not think the window 'quite so good'; this implies a comparison ('as good as you said', 'as good as York Minster', or whatever). He talks of 'the vault'; this means that a vault has been mentioned, or something which is known by both speaker and hearer to have a vault. He asks why B did not tell him about it; this carries the implication that B could, or should, have done so.

It is into this field of meaning that Chomsky's pupils wandered in the early seventies. But where exactly did they think they were heading?

§123. Are such things part of an intrinsic meaning of sentences? It is not evident that they are.

Take just the meaning of *the vault*. In our conversation it is understood with reference to the cathedral, *the cathedral* having been likewise understood with reference to Exeter. In another conversation A and B might both be standing in the building; then it is understood with reference to their surroundings. But is the speaker bound to mean it that way? Suppose another vault has come into his head, and he refers to that instead. Perhaps he will be misunderstood. But this is again a matter of how sentences are taken in context. In principle the utterance could refer to any vault whatever – that is, to anything to which the word *vault* can be applied.

By talking of SRs the generative semanticists invited criticism of this sort. For extended illustration see, for instance, Kempson's monograph on presuppositions [59].

§124. The natural answer is to reject intrinsic SRs. The only meaning of a sentence is the one it has in the particular context of utterance.

This is no novel theory. For de Saussure [32] the sentence was a unit only of 'parole'. So too for Gardiner, whose *Theory of Speech and Language* [60] is especially important. It is in such a view that generative semantics has perhaps begun to find its rationale – precisely in rejecting generative notions.

But utterance meaning does not stop where we want to stop. In Chafe's example, the speaker's brain was said to contain the configuration of concepts 'It is raining' (§120). But is that all that was in his mind? Perhaps he sounded glad; it gave him an excuse to stay indoors until it was over. Or perhaps he sounded annoyed; he has to go out and he has mislaid his mackintosh. Or again he is glad; it is because he has mislaid it that he has an excuse for staying in. Such accounts can be extended; see Gardiner's discussion (ibid., pp. 71*ff*.) of a similar example.

Of course this is not what Chafe was after. He wanted to abstract a sentence *It is raining* and say that it means 'It is raining'. But that is not a matter of thoughts that arise on the occasion.

§125. Let us return to the conversation about cathedrals (§122). Again there is much more we might say about the meanings of these utterances.

The man from Devon asked A to 'forgive' his local patriotism. Now A is the sort of Yorkshireman who does go on about his native county; B feels that he can be forgiven for replying in kind. In his heart he knows that he goes on a bit too; but he feels that for once it was justified. And what is wrong with local pride anyway? He does not see it as something one can object to. All this is reflected in the words he used: *you must forgive*, not simply *that was due to*, or *you must not condemn*, and so forth. It is also clear to B. He does not take this as a real request for pardon, or as stating an obligation to grant it.

Earlier B asked if A 'had time' for the cathedral. He knew that A was in a hurry; hence *Did you have time . . .?* not just *Did you visit . . .?* He also knows that A has no real interest in stained glass – except when bragging about Yorkshire. Yet A would not have mentioned Exeter unless he was going to say something on this topic. This too is understood between them.

The more we continue the more detailed our descriptions get. But surely these are not matters that we, as linguists, are concerned with.

§126. "Quite so. Our job is to describe the language system, not the meaning of utterances in performance. This system forms the speaker's competence. So, we have to ask what that competence consists of.

"You referred to de Saussure (§124). But in a Saussurean theory only the word or morpheme is a unit of 'la langue'; only such elements enter into systematic oppositions of meaning. Surely we cannot retreat into that hole."

I certainly do not wish to do so.

"But neither does 'la langue' account for every property of utterance meaning. Indeed it could never be exhausted. We could never say that this – all and only this – is what the speaker meant by his utterance."

Agreed.

"So, we are concerned with just some properties. Then what are they? Obviously, they are what Chomsky calls intrinsic meanings. That is the only alternative to the morass in which the generative semanticists are plunging."

§127. I would, of course, suggest another alternative. The language system is again established by a process of cutting and smoothing (§8). We must try and state the principles on which it is done, just as, for example, we would investigate the principles of dictionary-writing (§§6, 114). But we should not pretend that such a system has been internalised by the speaker.

This is in line with our earlier discussion of the sentence (§§50–5), and with the approach of Lyons's *Semantics* [30], which I referred to. The argument with our objector must take essentially the same course as before.

§128. Let us begin with an apparently routine example, illustrating what are fashionably called implicatures.

It is summer and A is walking along the street. B comes up to him and asks: *Please, is there anywhere I can get some ice cream?* Now A will not simply answer *Yes*. Nor, if they are in Reading, will he say: *You might try somewhere on Blackpool seafront.* Nor can he reasonably say: *You'll have to pay for it, you know.*

Instead A may reply: *I think there's a greengrocer's just round the corner.* B will not then ask: *What has that got to do with it?* Instead he will say *Thank you* and walk off in the direction in which A is pointing.

Some of this might be explained by general principles of conversation. Under such principles B's question will be taken to mean: 'If so, please where is it?' Likewise A's answer will be taken to imply: 'I think the greengrocer sells ice cream.' This reflects assumptions made by the hearer (A assumes B had some motive for asking; B assumes that A is trying to help him), which would be made whatever language was being spoken. Such explanations are on the same level as our tentative account of hesitation (§40).

Some may be explained by other aspects of our culture. We would not find it surprising that a greengrocer should sell ice cream. (What if A had said *There's a bank just round the corner?*) To get ice cream we do assume that we will have to pay for it. This too has nothing to do with either speaker's competence in English.

But exactly how much does have a linguistic explanation? Suppose B fails to say *please*; to get A's attention he just approaches him and looks him in the face. Now that would be less polite – a reflection, we cannot but say, of the meaning of *please*. Then suppose that B says simply: *I want a shop that sells ice cream.* By conversational principles this too could be taken as a request for information. But A could more reasonably tell him to get lost. Why so?

§129. We can compare B's question with some other, more clear-cut examples.

Battalion will parade at 1700 – does this have the SR of a statement? Only it is taken, under 'language independent' principles, to implicate a command? What rubbish! It is simply the normal linguistic formula in such a context.

A: *Can I play scrum-half?* B: *No, you can play full-back because I'm having Peter as scrum-half* – have these the SRs of a question followed by a statement, both concerned with A's ability to play in these positions? Only they are understood, by general principles, as a request and a direction? Surely not. It is not surprising that a modal expressing ability should also have such other meanings. But that it has is still a feature of the particular language.

Now, if John could stand there . . . and Mary, would you like to stand next to the bride? – does this have the SR of an unfinished conditional, followed by a question about Mary's preference? Only the conditional will conversationally imply: 'If so, that's what I want you to do'? And the question implies: 'Unless you've got any objection, stand there'? No, this too is inadequate. Suppose, for example, that the speaker had said *provided* instead of *if*: *Now, provided John could stand there.* Let us also substitute *enjoy* for *like*: *and Mary, would you enjoy standing next to the bride?* Well, that is not very polite to the bride, is it?

Evidently the *if* is not intrinsically a part of a conditional. Nor has *like* its full import. They are parts of conventional formulae for making requests or giving directions.

Now let us look again at the way B asked about ice cream. Was it really interpreted by independent principles? Or is it another formula, appropriate to that sort of request? It is not obvious that either is entirely right.

§130. The problem is highlighted in an honest book by Sadock [61], which I have recently reviewed [62].

Sadock points out that there are many formulae; they are like idioms and must have SRs appropriate to their use. But his theory allows for only one SR at a time. Any instance must be either intrinsically idiomatic, like the command *Battalion will parade . . .*, or intrinsically non-idiomatic, like the statement *The battalion paraded . . .* Sadock wonders if the theory will hold.

It seems clear that it will not. Suppose B had asked: *Please, can you tell me if there is anywhere I can get some ice cream?* Again A could not reasonably answer *Yes.* But he could reasonably answer *No*, or *I'm afraid I can't.* In that case he is taking it as an unidiomatic question. Now suppose B had asked: *Please, can I find out from you if there is anywhere . . .?* But surely an English speaker would not say that. *Can you tell me . . .* must be a formula for requests, which *Can I find out from you . . .* is not. On this evidence *Can you tell me . . .* is *ad libitum* both idiomatic and non-idiomatic.

§131. In general, there is no precise typology of speech acts (requests, statements, and so on). If we try to find one we will merely make our judgement dizzy.

Of course, there are plenty of easy examples. *Stand back, please!* is a command or order (said, say, by a policeman at the scene of an accident). We have already had a clear-cut request: *Can I play scrum-*

half? Then there are questions (*Who will be coming?*), statements, and so on.

But easy examples are so often deceptive. *Please give us a bit more room* – again an order, would you say? Or has it just a touch of a request about it? (Suppose our policeman said it; would it carry quite the same authority?) *Could you please move over a little?* – is that just a politer form of order? (Certainly it is not designed to elicit the answer *No*). *I wonder if I could possibly squeeze in here, could I?* – here there is another formula (try saying *I'm asking myself whether . . .*), but for what precisely? Maybe we will feel that it is even more 'request-like' – or does that just mean that it is even more polite? Take off the tag: *I wonder if I could possibly squeeze in here.* Does that make it less of a request? If so, what is it more of? Try the second person instead of the first: *I wonder if you could possibly move over a little, could you?* Do you feel that this helps you at all to think of it as an order? Try something blunter: *I think I can squeeze in here, can't I?* Now do you think it is getting more 'question-like'? *You couldn't possibly move over, could you please?* – well, at least we have left orders behind. But completely behind?

We can start again from our second easy example. *Could I perhaps play scrum-half?* – again a request, only more hesitant. *Would you mind letting me play scrum-half?* – this too is formulaic (try saying *Would you be annoyed at having to let me play scrum-half?*), but is it not a shade more 'question-like'? (Would it be quite so appropriate to answer *Yes, of course you can?*) *Would you like to have me as scrum-half?* – can we say that this is yet more of a 'question'? Or is it more like an offer? (Compare *Would you like another glass of sherry?*) *Is there any chance of me playing scrum-half?* – Hasn't this still the ghost of a request left in it?

By all means try and fit these into an exhaustive classification. But promise to try again in a week or so's time. Do you think you would be likely to agree with all your earlier judgements?

§132. So far I have avoided the term 'pragmatics', as its sense is too fluid. But if *semantics* has to do with Chomsky's intrinsic meanings (§100), *pragmatics* must deal with whatever meanings are not intrinsic. So, what we are denying is that semantics and pragmatics have a natural boundary.

By the seventies Chomsky himself appears to have doubts. In

1967 intrinsic meanings had a status which was 'obvious'; see again his appendix to Lenneberg [45]. A few years later we are asked to 'assume' that such a theory 'makes sense' (paper for the Hattori Festschrift [63], also in *Studies on Semantics* . . . [6], p. 183). But we should also read a lecture of about the same time [64], which is printed in the second edition of *Language and Mind*. Here Chomsky admits (p. 111):

> In fact the notion 'representation of meaning' or 'semantic representation' is . . . highly controversial. It is not clear at all that it is possible to distinguish sharply between the contribution of grammar to the determination of meaning, and the contribution of so-called 'pragmatic considerations', questions of fact and belief and context of utterance.

It is not in Chomsky's nature to cry 'peccavi'. But surely this comes pretty near to it.

§133. Is there any other point at which semantics and pragmatics can be divided? I fear that many scholars will fall over backwards to propose one.

"But is it so very difficult? The speaker has internalised a grammar, as we said. It is this, and only this, that specifies intrinsic meanings. But perhaps he also has some form of pragmatic competence. It is for that, and not for the grammar, that your problems of demarcation will arise.

"The pragmatic rules are part of what we called communicative competence (§44). With other factors, they determine the *communicative meaning* of a sentence. At this level the boundaries of competence may well be indeterminate. It was difficult to state limits in the field of language and culture (tribe B in §43). Perhaps it is also difficult in the field of speech acts. I would not be astonished if, in marginal cases, we would indeed be forced to cut and smooth.

"But neither would I be worried. For communicative or pragmatic competence has no connection with the intrinsic meanings which we have postulated. We must think of these as *cognitive meanings*, quite removed from any communicative use. The communicative meaning of a sentence may on occasion be very different from the cognitive meaning which the grammar assigns to it.

"So what have you shown? At most, that certain rules of use may not have a precise characterisation. Well, so what? It is the basic cognitive system that a generative grammar is concerned with. Against that you have said nothing."

§134. My objector's remarks are more pointed than anything I have yet read in the literature. Nor am I certain how far Chomsky would endorse them (§45). But I can think of examples which such a model might seem to illuminate.

Suppose we are soldiers standing to attention on the parade ground. The sergeant major gives the order: *Parade, slope arms!* We accordingly slope arms. Then, in the same way, he bellows out: *Parade, remove boots!* What do we do? There is no way of taking off our boots by numbers (One – bend down – two three – grasp the end of right bootlace, and so on). And what are we supposed to do with our rifles meanwhile? I am afraid we may well think that he has taken leave of his senses.

This gaffe might now be explained as follows. As a sentence *Parade, remove boots!* has its SR just as we would expect: it is an order to people on parade to take off their boots. That would be its intrinsic meaning. But as an utterance it was communicatively null; there are pragmatic constraints, internalised to some degree by every English speaker, which exclude it as a formal military command. In another situation it might be meaningful. (*Parade, stand at ease! – Stand easy!* – then, in the same 'Stand easy' tone of voice, *Sit down!* – then, still more jocularly, *Parade, remove boots!*) But, as given, it had no pragmatic or communicative interpretation. That is why, as soldiers, we could not respond to it.

§135. If pragmatic rules can exclude interpretations, our objector will also want them to be added.

"Consider once more the formula with *if*: *Now, if John could stand there*. You maintained that this could not be a conditional; it had to have the SR of a direction (§129). But your argument is not convincing. In the grammar it is indeed an *if*-clause. It is part of a complex sentence, which expresses an implication between propositions. It is only by a pragmatic rule that such a clause takes on a directive value."

By such shifts we could limit SRs to the specification of truth conditions, or whatever else was thought to be manageable. There are many writers who yearn to restrict semantics in that way.

§136. What would be the arguments against this model? First, I still have problems in delimiting intrinsic meanings.

Take the request with *can*: thus *Can I play scrum-half?* Is *can* ambiguous in the cognitive system, so that the SR will already have an epistemic sense? Or is the cognitive *can* restricted to the sense of ability? So that the other senses are given only in pragmatics?

"Presumably they are distinguished in the cognitive system, since they can yield different truth values."

Then what would be its SR as a whole? Is it intrinsically a yes/no question? ('Is it or is it not the case that my playing scrum-half is permitted?')

"That seems a likely hypothesis."

But its natural use is as a request. (Suppose one replied *I'll have to look on the noticeboard*; that would mean 'to see if I can grant what you are asking', not 'to find out if it is the case'.) So on what grounds would an interrogative SR be justified? Only in forced usage, if at all, does the sentence mean what this representation of its meaning says it means.

"Then perhaps it is intrinsically a request."

But now we are back on the skids. For if the grammar can specify requests in the form of interrogatives, why not directions in the form of protases (*Now, if John . . .*), requests in the form of declaratives (*I wonder if . . .*), and so on? Once more we would not know where to stop.

Do I seem a trifle at sea? Indeed I am. For this sort of model offers no more than a terminology. It proposes distinctions, but no criteria by which they could be realised.

§137. A second problem is that of learning. How do speakers come to acquire two different sorts of competence?

A child learns to talk – that is, to communicate – in English. In Chomskyan terms, he acquires rules which will be reflected in his communicative performance. They are constructed on the evidence of other speakers' utterances: so, from the way that they themselves communicate.

But some of these are treated separately. They form a cognitive system, which is merely used for communicative purposes. Then is there separate evidence on which they are constructed? No. Their basis too is in other speakers' utterances: again, in the way that they communicate.

Then why should such a system be isolated? Why is not every rule a communicative rule?

§138. "But that is simply the way the human mind is organised. A child has a special device for grammar construction – what Chomsky calls the LAD. This develops his cognitive competence, or what we earlier called the faculty of grammar (see again §44). He also has a general faculty of communication; this is a different faculty of the mind, which develops on separate principles. That is what constructs his communicative competence, or what we earlier called the rules of speaking (§47). The rules are separate precisely because these are separate faculties."

In short, we can only say he does it if we also say he is genetically programmed to do it.

§139. My colleague has tried to tell me *why* a learner should make this separation. But he has still not told me *how*.

Let us take two children in the same community, learning the language from the same set of adults. Would their grammars generate the same set of sentences?

"Presumably they would."

So, in particular, they would make the same division between communicative and cognitive competence?

"Of course. Otherwise their cognitive systems would not match."

Then what ensures that they do so? How is the division determined from their evidence?

We are dealing with an anthropomorphic mind, so let us speak anthropomorphically. Is there some rationale by which these faculties sort out facts between them? ('Ah! This bit is my pigeon' – 'No. Surely it is mine' – 'Nonsense! It is obviously of my sort'.) The suggestion is absurd. The child has what Chomsky calls his 'primary linguistic data'. But in no sense is it divided into 'data for the construction of communicative rules' and 'data for the construction of cognitive rules'.

Is the grammar determined, in the end, on other evidence? But what other evidence could there be? An English speaker learns the grammar of English – not of French, or German, and so on. How can he do it, if not on the basis of English speech?

§140. These remarks elaborate an argument of Strawson's, which he applies to any non-communicative view of language. (See the end of his inaugural lecture [65].) Perhaps it is wasted on this particular proposal.

Yet the proposal is worth knocking down. For if the grammar cannot be restricted in that fashion (§§133–5), it is hard to see how we could hold back from the problems which the generative semanticist is putting before us. For they are the real problems of meaning, morass though they may be (end of §126).

RULES AND TENDENCIES

§141. In Chomsky's thesis, to know a language is to know a set of rules. There are rules for every aspect of language: for syntax, for phonetic representations, for the meanings of individual words, for the meanings of combinations of words, and so on. The language system is *fully codified*, providing a code, or system of rules, that underlies all facets of performance.

In our thesis, the language system is only *partly codified*. A form such as *purpleness* is neither right nor wrong (§28); there is no rule by which that question could be decided. It is neither right nor wrong to apply the word *pin* to a part of my bicycle padlock (§110); the use of such a word is not precisely constrained. It would be neither right nor wrong for my shepherd to use a standard form (§78); it would merely be less usual. For these aspects of performance no rule can be stated.

But where there is no rule there may often be a regularity. We find a general pattern by which countables are used uncountably (§§32–4); perhaps this is especially strong for nouns of certain classes. This pattern we called a *tendency*. Likewise there is a tendency by which nouns will be formed in -*ness*, a tendency for nouns such as *stillness* not to be the subject of verbs such as *kill* (§102), and so on.

The term 'tendency' is taken from an important article by Haas ('Meanings and rules' [66]). In this view languages are constituted partly by tendencies – so only partly by rules.

§142. Rules are characteristic of syntax. But syntactic constructions are realised by individual words. It is in this interaction of construction and collocation that the limits of rules are shown most clearly.

An obvious case is where two regularities exist in conflict. One could be presented as a rule; but then the other must be seen as a tendency to break it. A notorious instance is in the factors governing subject-verb agreement. So let us briefly review it.

§143. One factor is inflectional number: thus *The children paint*, not *The children paints*. Co-ordination is another: thus, *John and Jenny paint*. In both examples *paints* would be wrong. We can express this by the traditional rule: singular or simple subject with singular, plural or co-ordinate subject with plural.

But then there is the notional factor. We can say *The entire board has resigned*, but also *The entire board have . . . .* We could say *The form and interpretation of this schema are as follows*. But we can also say *The form and interpretation . . . is . . .*, and I have myself written *The form and the interpretation . . . is . . . .* Such examples show a different regularity: notionally singular subjects with singular, notionally plural with plural. But how does it tie in with the first? Is there any principle which will resolve the conflict between them?

It is of interest that even Fowler shrank from laying down a rule. With the co-ordinate subject I would indeed have been told off ([67], s.v. Number, §2). But not in the case of *board*: 'In general, it may be said that while there is always a better & a worse in the matter, there is seldom a right and a wrong, & any attempt to elaborate rules would be waste labour' (ibid., §5). What can we add – except that in many examples it is not clear that there is even a better and a worse?

§144. "But we can easily have rules which, in isolation, would have contrary effects. In the grammar one might be ordered before the other. Then perhaps the earlier might be optional, or the later might be able (optionally) to reverse its application.

"Is not something like this the solution here? As you have said,

The board have . . . is neither better nor worse, in general, than *The board has* . . . . Here either rule could apply, so that both results would be grammatical. In other cases only one could operate. For *The children paint*, it must be the rule of grammatical concord: as you say, *The children paints* is ungrammatical. Conceivably there are cases where it must be the rule of notional concord. Then the sentence with the strict agreement would be ungrammatical. There might also be cases where the choice of one rule or the other carries a difference of meaning.

"The only problem then is to determine the precise conditions under which each rule applies."

But it is just that that is the snag. For how can we find precise conditions? How do we limit what is grammatical and ungrammatical?

§145. Let me invite the reader to look at borderline instances.

One can say *The printing and the binding of books are* . . . . But now miss out the second article: *The printing and binding of books are getting very expensive*. Would one use the plural here? It is the sort of correction one might perhaps get from a pedantic sub-editor. Take a more homely example: *Even their fish and chips are getting expensive*. I think one would normally say *is*, but would *are* be ungrammatical? In these cases I am not sure if I can appropriately follow Fowler's rule. But neither am I quite sure how far I can break it. What about, say, *Eggs and chocolate sauce doesn't go together*? I feel it would be better with *don't*; nevertheless it is a great deal more acceptable than *John and Jenny paints*.

Turning to simple subjects, one can certainly say *The remainder have been burnt*. But what about *The residue have been burnt* or *The remaining part have been burnt*? Both strike me as doubtful; yet they are much better than, let us say, *The wood have been burnt*. Why so, if sentences are equally grammatical or equally ungrammatical? Perhaps some readers will be more influenced by the notional factor. Then would they be as happy with, for example, *The cat population have grown smaller*? For a reverse example, would one say *The leftovers has been destroyed*? I have the feeling that I do not, but it is by no means as bad as *The trees has been destroyed*.

If we explored this further we would discover many complications. Quirk and his colleagues point to a third factor of proximity

(*Grammar of Contemporary English* [2], p. 360): thus *Everything, even the chips, are ready.* So, in his rather different way, did Fowler ([67], s.v. Number, §4). Then there is certainly stylistic variation. These factors we can leave aside, as none of them will help the generativist's case.

§146. "But surely Chomsky himself has proposed a scale of grammaticalness? Let us imagine three sentences *x*, *y* and *z*. Perhaps *x* is grammatical, while both *y* and *z* are ungrammatical. Nevertheless *y* may still be more acceptable than *z*: that is, if *y* shows more points of similarity with *x*. Once again, your problems lie outside the grammar's field of explanation."

This invokes a proposal of which we have heard little in the past twelve years. I do not know if Chomsky still thinks it is on. But in fact he only posited a scale of ungrammaticalness: between *x*, which is grammatical, and *y*, which is merely acceptable, there is still a distinction. How can we decide where it lies, or explain why learners should make it?

My objector's argument is a variant of one raised earlier for formations in -*ness* (§29). A further shift might be one involving idiolectal multilingualism (§27). But we have learned by now that we cannot rescue such boundaries by drawing them more narrowly.

§147. Notional concord is a tendency of rather general scope. But rules can deal with limited exceptions; could a tendency also do so?

Examples are again before our eyes, provided we are willing to see them. There is an awkwardness, for instance, in some combinations of auxiliaries. We can say *I am being seen*, *I have been seen*; but can we also say *I have been being seen*? We can say *I am being foolish*, *I have been foolish*; but can we also say *I have been being foolish*? Now we do tend to avoid such sequences. But are they flatly excluded? *This house has been being built for twenty years* – any observant scholar will be familiar with examples of this kind. There seem no grounds to posit a rule which states that they are ungrammatical.

Some transformationalists might speak of a surface structure constraint; the deep structures are generated but their surface reflexes are blocked. Fine, but why call it a constraint? In a paper on collocations Bazell has distinguished *constraint*, by rule, from *re*straint, which is by what we are calling tendencies [68]. Here, too, speakers are *re*strained from a certain pattern. But they are not *con*strained by a rule forbidding it absolutely.

§148. In what other circumstances must a partial codification be recognised? So far we have been dealing with an indeterminacy in grammaticalness. A more interesting case is where there is an indeterminacy in interpretation. On one view, *x* might be construed on the pattern of *a*, *b* and *c*. On another, it might be construed on that of *p*, *q* and *r*. Yet *x* is not ambiguous. There is just no way of saying which pattern, or which regularity, it comes under.

In such cases Bolinger has spoken of *syntactic blends*: the first example which follows (§149) is modelled on his paper of that title [69]. The argument is clarified and reinforced in a more recent study by Palmer [70].

§149. *Mary is particularly nice to dance with* – what exactly does this mean? Does it mean, perhaps, that 'dancing with Mary' is 'particularly nice' ('a particularly nice thing to do')? If so, a transformationalist might posit an underlying structure as follows:

[[X dances with Mary] is particularly nice.]

This would be an impersonal interpretation.

Or does it mean that 'Mary is particularly nice', 'for dancing with' or 'when one dances with her'? If so, its underlying structure might instead be like this:

[Mary is particularly nice [X dances with Mary].]

That would be a personal interpretation.

If the sentence is impersonal it is like, for example, *He is easy to please, That tree will be difficult to cut down, Mary is the easiest girl to get to know*. If it is personal it is like, for example, *He is getting heavy to lift, That radiator will be rather hot to sit on, Mary is an impressionable girl to talk to*. Well, which is it? The answer is that it is neither definitely one nor definitely the other. There is a blending or fusing of the two semantic patterns.

§150. Let us now take a case that has emerged since Bolinger's article. It is again one which, at first sight, the generative school appeared to handle well.

He promises to be a great violinist – this is, of course, ambiguous. It may mean that he 'has made a promise' to become one; if so it might have a personal structure as follows:

[He promises [he will be . . .].]

Alternatively, it may mean that 'it looks as if' he will become one. For this some writers have proposed an impersonal structure – something like:

[[He will be . . .] promises.]

In one case we understand it to be like *He wants to be a great violinist*: this is something 'he wants' to be. In the other it is like *He happened to be a great violinist*: that is, 'it so happened' that he was. A very clear exposition can be found in Ruwet's application to French [71].

§151. So far no trouble. But it is notorious that *begin*, for example, causes difficulties.

John began to read the book – well, this sounds like a positive act on John's part. (We can see how that sense would be lost in the passive: *The book began to be read by John, The book began to be read*.) So, it has been suggested, we must posit a personal structure:

[John began [John read . . .].]

Then take another sentence: *The tree-roots began to ruin the lawn*. This seems more like something that 'begins to happen'. (And here there is no discrepancy with the passive: *The lawn began to be ruined, The lawn began to be ruined by tree-roots*.) So, it is suggested, this must have the impersonal structure:

[[The tree-roots ruined . . .] began.]

There is no volition on the part of the tree-roots.

It is proposed, then, that there are two constructions as with *promise*. But where does one start and the other end? *Many people are beginning to discuss this book* – is this something 'they are beginning' to do, or something that is 'beginning to come about'? The sense does not seem to be lost in the passive: *Your book is beginning to be discussed, It is beginning to be discussed by many people*. Does that show that the construction is impersonal? But then is the subject not of the volitional sort? *Even her husband is beginning to dislike her* – perhaps we will say that this is something he is 'doing'. But let us add a personal type of adverb to the passive: *She has very foolishly begun to get disliked even by her own husband.* Could one not say that?

In the end, it is misleading to give definite answers. Constructions with *begin* are neither wholly personal nor wholly impersonal. They belong to the no man's land between two tendencies of interpretation.

§152. "Very well, we cannot plump exclusively for either structure. But that is simply a definition of ambiguity. Take the example with *nice* (§149). It can be construed, you would say, on either pattern (§148). That means it has both structural descriptions."

Of course it does not mean that. With *promise* there was genuine ambiguity (§150). We can put the sentence in a concrete situation; we can show that this or that interpretation was intended. That is just what we cannot do in cases of blending. *Mary is exciting to look at* – in what circumstances would the speaker mean this personally or mean this impersonally?

"Well, if it is not ambiguous then it must be non-ambiguous. Either it has two structural descriptions or it has just one. To deny this is to deny that we can assign a clear syntactic description to the sentences of a language."

So, after all, it must be purely personal or purely impersonal? But either answer would be misleading. Each suppresses a part of the truth.

We can easily give a clear syntactic description. Namely, we have a subject (*Mary*), a copula (*is*), a predicative adjective (*particularly nice*) and its infinitival complement (*to dance with*). The same description could be given to both *John is easy to please* and *John is eager to please*.

Now we agree that this is not enough. For there are two semantic patterns, which with *easy* and *eager* can be sharply distinguished. The error is in supposing that such patterns are controlled by rule. With some adjectives one takes the structure one way, and with some the other. With some it may be ambiguous. But with many neither interpretation is compelling, and with some any choice would be wrong. Once more, we are dealing with regularities that are not subject to codification.

§153. I have avoided the term 'analogy', as it is one that Chomsky has consistently pooh-poohed. He cannot see that it has any useful sense.

For him that is indeed so. A child says *sprayed* or *roared* or *goed*, by analogy with other regular past tenses. In Chomskyan terms he has internalised a rule for that formation; 'by analogy' reduces to 'by rule'. Likewise for any other analogical patterning. If it is valid there must be a rule for it; so, there is nothing that a statement of analogy could add.

But in proposing such statements his opponents naturally reject that theory. A speaker may say *x* by analogy with one set of forms, or *y* by analogy with another; this means that there are regular patterns which are available to him. But it does not follow that they are constrained by rules – unless, by begging the question, one assumes that all things are constrained by rules.

"But this notion 'pattern of analogy' is very imprecise. All you are saying is that *a* is said on the pattern of *b*, then *b* on that of *c*, and so on. To explain why you are forced to say that the pattern is regular. Yet you refuse to state this regularity exactly."

I have tried to state the objection fairly. But we are reasoning on quite irreconcilable lines. For the exactness my objector wants is precisely that which we require of rules. It is only for some patterns that this order of exactness can be justified.

§154. I have argued that tendencies cannot be reduced to rules. But another possibility is the reverse: that rules are merely a special case of tendencies. A regularity, in general, may not have a definite domain of application. But certain regularities do, and by that token would constitute rules. This might perhaps be part of Hockett's thesis [4], that the whole of language can be reduced to patterns of analogy.

But different types of regularity may be explainable by different processes of learning. We begin to speak by a principle of *imitation*, mimicking forms we hear. That is a first stage of learning, which on its own is naturally not adequate. Then we also employ a principle of *analogy*, by which forms are analysed into patterns. A second stage of learning is to treat some patterns as productive, while suppressing others. It is that form of learning which gives rise to tendencies.

On its own that too would be inadequate. But then we employ a principle of *rationalisation*, by which tendencies are organised into a determinate system. This is a third stage of learning, and it is that form which accounts for rules.

Hockett's error (as I understand it) was to try and assimilate the third stage to the second – hence an unconvincing account of recursiveness. Chomsky's error is to try and assimilate the second to the third. It might be venial if the last stage led to total codification. But the second is never superseded, either in its effects or in its operation. Nor, strictly, is the first.

My 'stages' are successive levels of development, in Piaget's sense. (For a summary account see his *Biology and Knowledge* [72].) I see nothing psychologically improbable in such an account.

§155. The last stage justifies a generative grammar – a set of rules which constitute a generative grammar in sense 1 (§4). But its scope is severely restricted. It could give no account of word meaning, of lexical formations, of collocational restrictions, of speech acts, of notional agreement, of the interpretation of *He is easy to please*, and so on. It would be absurd to take it as a theory of the speaker's competence.

That is essentially the grammar of *Syntactic Structures* [8]. Chomsky's early work is often damaged by the accretions of the sixties.

§156. We might likewise justify his early notion of the sentence.

This is still in the tradition of Bloomfield's definition. For Bloomfield the sentence was a largest 'linguistic form': a 'form' not included, by virtue of linguistic patterning, in any more extensive 'form' (*Language* [73], p. 170). But what sort of patterning would establish sentences as we usually conceive them? The best answer is that they are the largest unit in which patterning is governed by rules. In Chomsky's terms, a system of rules will take S, for sentence, as its initial category.

Of the later theorists Harris is particularly important. His starting point is in utterances: a 'language or dialect . . . comprises the talk which takes place in a language community . . .' (*Methods* [74], p. 13). These terms cannot be 'rigorously defined'. But at the end of his book we reach a passage which leads clearly into Chomsky's theory. Thus:

The work of analysis leads right up to the statements which

enable anyone to synthesize or predict utterances in the language. These statements form a deductive system with axiomatically defined initial elements and with theorems concerning the relationships among them. The final theorems would indicate the structure of the utterances of the language in terms of the preceding parts of the system. (ibid., pp. 372–3)

A generative system is the logical conclusion of the distributional method.

Harris says nothing of sentences, here or effectively elsewhere. But with hindsight it is easy to put two and two together. An utterance is a sequence of one or more Bloomfieldian sentences. That is, of forms within which there is linguistic patterning. To synthesise an utterance is to synthesise such a sequence. But between sentences there is no such patterning. In Chomskyan terms, there are no rules which operate. So, the synthesis may start with each S individually. Here we have the source of Chomsky's *initial string* $(S_1, S_2 \ldots S_n)$, from which potential utterances, or sequences of sentences, were derived.

That is historically the basis for a generative account of syntax, or of grammar in the traditional sense. I stress its essentially Bloomfieldian inspiration.

§157. Bloomfield's definition was presented with a marvellous air of chucking out traditional nonsense (see his review of Ries's book, in particular [75]). But it also chucked out any serious discussion of sentence meaning. The problems remained buried, for most North American linguists, until the generative semanticists unwittingly dug them up again.

It was on to such a theory of the sentence (or such a lack of a theory of the sentence) that Katz and Fodor's semantic component [47] had to be grafted. But how could they be made compatible?

A Harrisian utterance (U) was a string of Chomskyan, or Bloomfieldian, sentences $(S_1, S_2 \ldots S_n)$. The semantic component assigned a meaning to each sentence; so, just as the syntactic structure of U was the sum of the syntactic structures of S_i, the meaning of U would be synthesised or 'predicted' (§156) as the sum of the meanings of S_i. But that will plainly not do. In Bloomfield's example the speaker uttered the sentence *It's a fine day* ([75], loc. cit.); that is one

S to which the semantic component must assign an interpretation. He then said *Are you going to play tennis this afternoon?* – that is another S. As linguistic forms, or as grammatical structures, they are separate. But in meaning they form a whole. The interpretation of an utterance or text is always greater than the sum of those assignable to its parts.

How else might syntax and semantics be integrated? One way is to sacrifice the former to the latter. Semantic theory is developed into a genuine theory of communication; syntax becomes a merely realisational component; its generative treatment must be abandoned. That is the road eventually taken by generative semantics.

Another is the road that Chomsky himself took in the early to middle sixties. The grammar still assigns a syntactic structure to each S; to each S it also assigns a semantic interpretation. But neither the S nor its meaning can be instanced directly in an utterance. Both must be mental objects, quite abstracted from performance. Hence the mentalist account of *Aspects* [7], where generative grammar is enlarged into an account of competence. The extension is quite foreign to his earliest writings.

§158. What do I myself suggest? Above all, that we should not try to convert a grammar into an integrated theory of a language. If grammars are limited to grammar we can treat that aspect of language as it deserves, and other aspects as they deserve.

This brings us back to the spirit of my introduction (§§10 and following).

GRAMMAR AND MIND

§159. We have often had to skirt the edge of wider philosophical issues. An obvious instance was at the beginning of our discussion of competence (§§37–8); we could scarcely assume our adversary's theory of knowledge. But in the end it is to that point that our controversy must return. We attack his theory of competence by arguing that, in practice, speakers cannot know a language that way. He will defend it by arguing that, in principle, it is the only way a speaker's knowledge of a language can be conceived.

I am not a philosopher, and by my training am ill qualified to try to be one. But there are certain commonplaces which an amateur may be permitted to repeat. There is also a sense in which our arguments may be of philosophical interest. Chomsky has a certain philosophy of mind, Cartesian except that he recoils from dualism. One might easily suppose that this could be supported from his findings in linguistics. A philosopher might therefore defer to his expertise. But it is quite the opposite. His findings in linguistics, or his doctrines in linguistics, merely reflect his philosophy.

§160. I remarked in passing that our generativist had an anthropomorphic concept of the mind (§139). I hope no reader thought this unfair. In *Aspects* [7] Chomsky draws explicit parallels between an innate faculty of language and a linguist who is constructing and evaluating a grammar. If that is not anthropomorphism I do not know what would be.

"Heavens! Can't you recognise a metaphor when you see one? Look, a man behaves in a certain way. There must be something that controls his behaviour: in plain English, his mind. Part of his behaviour is linguistic behaviour; so, there must be a part of his mind that controls that in particular. We call this his linguistic competence, and our description of it we call a generative grammar. But where does this competence come from? Obviously, his mind must acquire it, and the part of the mind acquiring it is what we call the faculty of language.

"So, the linguist writes (or constructs) a generative grammar; the faculty of language acquires (or constructs) the speaker's competence; the generative grammar describes the speaker's competence. That is all you are being asked to accept. That given, what is wrong with a little harmless transference of terms?"

Of course this is just what I mean by anthropomorphism. There is something there that sits at the wheel and makes the man do what he does. To do this the something must have acquired the art of driving. We can arrive at hierarchies of angels that way.

§161. How else might my colleague try to make me understand his position? I think he would return to his comparisons with physical sciences (§§4–5).

"You spoke at one point of a formal language as a model for a real language (§19). Likewise we see a formal grammar as a model for one part of the speaker's mind. Now scientists make models of other things: for instance, of the solar system. We ask what that system is like. That can only mean: what is our present understanding of it? In answer, we propose a model which, on our present evidence, appears to be the best available. It is just the same with grammars. Our model of the speaker's competence is simply our best understanding of what it is that makes him speak as he does."

It is important to appreciate the fudging in this last remark. 'A grammar is a model of the speaker's competence' – if that makes sense the rest is unexceptionable. But that is precisely the point: can we talk of 'making models of the mind' in the same way that we talk of modelling the physical universe?

§162. Let us take a rather hackneyed sort of parallel. We fall in love because, let us say, the goddess of love has picked us out for treatment. So, we try to understand the goddess. We advance the hypothesis that she is particularly active in the spring; we can see if there is statistical evidence which will support it. We ask why so many people fall in love with X; we try to predict whether the goddess will also work so powerfully through Y. In this way we can surely be said to develop a theory or model. Our model of Aphrodite, we would say, is simply our best understanding of what it is that makes people fall in love.

Of course, she has many characteristics that are poorly understood. Like the science of linguistics, the science of Aphroditistics is very much in its infancy. But give us time, give us time!

§163. "I am afraid you evidently need some more lessons in the philosophy of science. Look, when we propose a model of the solar system it is naturally a part of our hypothesis that such a thing exists. In principle this might be wrong: that is, the hypothesis could be disproved. We also assume that the system can be described in isolation. That too is falsifiable. All this conforms to the normal canon of a scientific theory.

"Now let us return to Aphrodite. Would she herself be part of a hypothesis? Then how would one disprove it? What evidence could possibly convince us that she does not exist? Of course there

is no hypothesis at all. The goddess of love is a mere personification –
just like 'Nature', for example. These are things that scientists have
long learned to do without.

"Obviously, when a linguist proposes his competence model he
is not doing anything like that. The notion 'competence' is itself
part of our theory, and we expect it to be evaluated accordingly."

Unfortunately, that is just what is not obvious. 'A speaker's mind
has developed a linguistic competence' – in what way is this a
falsifiable statement? What would be admitted as evidence against
it? Here our generativist has to face the problems that we began to
raise in §22. He will not allow his hypothesis to be falsified by mere
performance. Then are we dealing with a notion on which evidence
can be brought to bear (§15)?

§164. "Then perhaps the existence o competence is something
that we simply take for granted – like the existence of the universe,
for example. Now you yourself may not be interested in making
a description of the speaker's mind. All you want to do is to describe
some aspects of his observable behaviour. Well, all right, we have
different goals. Let us just travel our different ways, and stop this
pointless arguing."

Here we have our reasonable man of §7. But we are trying to
find out if it is any real road that the generativist is travelling. 'We
are describing a part of the universe', 'We are describing a part of
an individual's mind', 'We are describing one of the gods that rule
us' – granted, Chomsky has made the second statement rather more
fashionable than the third. But how can it be parallel to the first?

§165. "Ah! Now I am beginning to see your problem. For some
reason you are terrified of making hypotheses about unobservables;
you feel that we cannot talk about the mind because the mind
cannot be examined to see if what we say is right. But what is there
to be frightened of? Other sciences do this; why should we refuse
to follow them?"

Of course this has nothing to do with it. The gods on Olympus
are also unobservable. Does that mean that it is legitimate to make
hypotheses about them?

§166. Our purpose is to try and clarify Chomsky's theory of mind.

Is it a rankly traditional theory, as I implied? If so, the arguments in these last few sections are just what we expect. A psychologist investigates a mental world just as the natural scientist investigates a physical world. The mind that inhabits this world has various parts, the faculty of language being among them. It is the job of the linguist to describe this or propose a model of it; that description or model is what we originally called a 'generative grammar in sense 2' (§4). If we cannot accept this, it is because we have been brainwashed by Skinner, or by Bloomfield, or by Ryle, or some other bogeyman.

I have the feeling that all this is rather scurrilous. But I find it hard to see any real alternative that Chomsky is offering us.

§167. At this point some objectors will begin to talk about the brain instead of the mind. 'Mind', we would be told, 'is no more than a traditional term. We know that it is in fact the brain that ultimately controls a man's activities. It is therefore the brain that forms the object of our model building.'

This is how many psychologists at first took it. A transformation, they supposed, was some sort of process that entered into the production and understanding of sentences. They devised experiments suggesting, for example, that a passive was more difficult to process than an active. Why so? Well, it was said, according to Chomsky's hypothesis the active would involve the phrase-structure rules alone, while the passive would require the same rules plus a transformation. Naturally, this is a much more complex process; hence their findings. So far as it went, this was supposed to confirm that transformational grammar was a correct model of the brain's operations.

But Chomsky soon made clear that this was not what he intended. A generative grammar is not a model for the generation of utterances; indeed it would be a bad one if it was. Nor does it model any other performance of that kind. How often has this been emphasised!

§168. "All right, it is not a model in any literal or direct sense. But at this point there is a fruitful analogy with computers. On the one hand the speaker has, let us say, a number of *performance programmes*: routines for producing an utterance, for assigning a semantic interpretation to an utterance, and so on. These are common to all men, whatever their language. On the other hand he has an *information store* with the rules of *his* language in particular – of English, of French, or whatever. The store is available as an input, we might say, to the performance programmes.

"Now let us consider the problem of acquisition. The performance programmes are innate: every child is born with the same wiring. So, if the large rectangle represents the brain as a whole, we can show this with a smaller rectangle as follows.

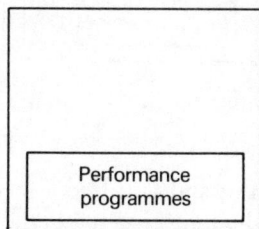

But, obviously, the particular information store is not innate; so let us show this with a blank box and a question mark.

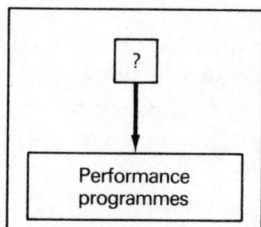

The store is provided for, but its contents are not yet specified. So what specifies them? Obviously, a further set of programmes that we have already called the LAD. So let us show this with a further rectangle.

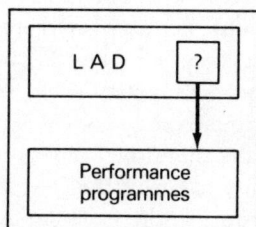

That means the LAD has the task of filling in the box with the question mark. The result we call the *grammar*; when that is complete the LAD will cease to function.

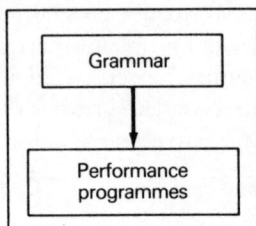

```
┌─────────────────────────┐
│   ┌─────────────────┐   │
│   │     Grammar     │   │
│   └─────────────────┘   │
│            │            │
│            ▼            │
│   ┌─────────────────┐   │
│   │   Performance   │   │
│   │   programmes    │   │
│   └─────────────────┘   │
└─────────────────────────┘
```

"There, we have spelled it out for you in simple diagrams. Now are you satisfied?"

§169. Scratch a mentalist and you find a mechanist. Are there the slightest grounds for thinking that the brain is organised in such a way?

"But it is our hypothesis that it is. Like any other hypothesis it is in play until it is proved false. If you would just read your Popper and so on . . ."

But what, once more, would be admitted as falsifying evidence? Our generativist would stick to his hypothesis through thick and thin. If he is ever knocked off it will be for other reasons.

"All right, but at least you must provide some arguments against it. What would they be?"

I would find it easier to answer if I knew what were supposed to be the arguments for it. Does one just assume that the brain is like a general purpose computer? So, it must be supplied with systems, programmes, blocks of memory, and so on in the way computer scientists would design them? And maybe with an assembler for converting rules of grammar into 'neuron language'? Now perhaps this last remark will seem particularly silly. Assembly languages are human constructs that are there to help a human user; in what sense could they have a biological counterpart? Well, let us think again of our objector's boxes. Why should one suppose that these have any better foundation?

Of course it is just the traditional theory in a new disguise. The reader will recall Ryle's myth of the 'ghost in the machine' [76]. The myth of the 'machine in the machine' is no improvement.

§170. "But surely it is at least an interesting question to consider how we might in principle construct some form of device which would be able to simulate a specific aspect of . . ."

Just so. The last refuge of the mentalist is in artificial intelligence.

§171. I said that 'some objectors' might wish to argue on these lines. It is perhaps less easy to connect them with Chomsky himself.

His early critics often connected his work with projects of machine translation. A generative grammar may be fit for a computer but not, they argued, for anything else. In answer, Chomsky has denied that he has any interests in that field. But is that really to the point? The first experiment in translation (the so-called 'Georgetown experiment') dates from 1954, Chomsky's major unpublished work from 1955 – are we to see this as a pure coincidence? Surely both belong to the same intellectual movement. In other subjects, the pioneers had just begun to think in computational terms: later, such ways of thinking were to reach an apogee in English-speaking universities of the sixties. We are now in the decade after the decades before. We can see that much of this was mere intoxication. Did not Chomsky's critics rightly sense this at the time?

What was so characteristic of this movement? At bottom is it not precisely that a man could draw a form of diagram like this

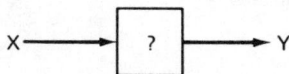

$$X \longrightarrow \boxed{?} \longrightarrow Y$$

and people would think it was a revealing way to formulate our kind of problem?

§172. Other times, other fashions. Chomsky's latest tack is to compare the faculty of language to a bodily organ.

As such it may be studied just like any other organ: 'an organ of vision, for example'. Likewise its development; we should not talk of someone learning a language – or even internalising its rules (§16)? – but rather of 'a person growing language in his head'. The words cited are from a lecture and discussion at Leiden, in December 1977. At the moment, my only published reference is to an interview with a Dutch weekly newspaper [77].

Perhaps I should not comment in advance of serious publication.

But all this seems to offer is a different metaphor. The old metaphor of a homunculus was scarcely less innocent.

§173. Such discussions have to go beyond banalities. On a philosophical level Chomsky's theory may still be kicking. But the argument has already gone beyond our discipline; these are not issues for linguistics, or even for the philosophy of language, but for the philosophy of mind in general. As students of language, we can show that our experience does not confirm what Chomsky said. That is the experience I have tried to survey in this book. But if our objector takes the line he took from §161 onwards, or earlier in §§4–5, we cannot answer him by our own methods.

Need that worry us? No. We have plenty of our own problems to mind. And if we mind those we will rediscover the genuine virtues of generative grammar, as one technique of linguistic description (§§11–14), which is especially appropriate for syntax (§§155–8), and not as a model of competence.

REFERENCES

[1] F. W. HOUSEHOLDER, 'Phonological theory: a brief comment', *Journal of Linguistics*, vol. 2 (1966), pp. 99–100.

[2] R. QUIRK, S. GREENBAUM, G. LEECH and J. SVARTVIK, *A Grammar of Contemporary English* (London, 1972).

[3] G. LAKOFF, 'Empiricism without facts', *Foundations of Language*, vol. 5 (1969), pp. 118–27.

[4] C. F. HOCKETT, *The State of the Art* (The Hague, 1968).

[5] J. D. MCCAWLEY, review of Chomsky [6] (available from Indiana University Linguistics Club).

[6] N. CHOMSKY, *Studies on Semantics in Generative Grammar* (The Hague, 1972).

[7] N. CHOMSKY, *Aspects of the Theory of Syntax* (Cambridge, Mass., 1965).

[8] N. CHOMSKY, *Syntactic Structures* (The Hague, 1957).

[9] C. E. BAZELL, *Linguistic Form* (Istanbul, 1953).

[10] P. H. MATTHEWS, review of Chomsky [7], *Journal of Linguistics*, vol. 3 (1967), pp. 119–52.

[11] R. E. LONGACRE, *Grammar Discovery Procedures* (The Hague, 1964).

[12] P. H. MATTHEWS. 'Some concepts in word and paradigm morphology', *Foundations of Language*, vol. 1 (1965), pp. 268–89.

[13] R. W. BURCHFIELD (ed.), *A Supplement to the Oxford English Dictionary*, Vol. 1, A–G, Vol. 2, H–N (Oxford, 1972, 1976).

[14] E. ARDENER (ed.), *Social Anthropology and Language* (London, 1971).

[15] C. F. HOCKETT, *Language, Mathematics and Linguistics* (The Hague, 1967).

[16] T. G. BEVER, 'The influence of speech performance on linguistic structure', in G. B. Flores d'Arcais and J. M. Levelt (eds), *Advances in Psycholinguistics* (Amsterdam, 1970), pp. 4–28.

[17] P. H. MATTHEWS, review of Hockett [4], *International Journal of American Linguistics*, vol. 37 (1971), pp. 49–52.

[18] S. C. DIK, 'Some critical remarks on the treatment of morphological structure in transformational generative grammar', *Lingua*, vol. 18 (1967), pp. 352–83.

[19] P. H. MATTHEWS, *Morphology* (London, 1974).

[20] JEAN BERKO, 'The child's learning of English morphology', *Word*, vol. 14 (1958), pp. 150–77.

[21] C. J. FILLMORE, 'On generativity', in S. Peters (ed.), *Goals of Linguistic Theory* (Englewood Cliffs, NJ, 1972).

[22] R. QUIRK, 'Descriptive statement and serial relationship', *Language*, vol. 41 (1965), pp. 205–17.

[23] D. CRYSTAL, 'English', in *Word Classes* (*Lingua*, vol. 17, nos 1–2, 1967), pp. 24–56.

[24] J. R. ROSS, 'A fake NP squish', in C.-J. N. Bailey and R. W. Shuy (eds), *New Ways of Analysing Variation in English* (Washington, DC, 1973), pp. 96–140.

[25] R. BROWN, *A First Language: the Early Stages* (Cambridge, Mass./London, 1973).

[26] D. HYMES, 'Sociolinguistics and the ethnography of speaking', in Ardener (ed.) [15], pp. 47–93.

[27] R. CAMPBELL and R. J. WALES, 'The study of language acquisition', in J. Lyons (ed.), *New Horizons in Linguistics* (Harmondsworth, 1970), pp. 243–60.

[28] D. CRYSTAL, *Prosodic Systems and Intonation in English* (Cambridge, 1969).

[29] W. DRESSLER, *Einführung in die Textlinguistik* (Tübingen, 1972).

[30] J. LYONS, *Semantics*, 2 vols (Cambridge, 1977).

[31] C. J. FILLMORE, 'A grammarian looks to sociolinguistics', in R. W. Shuy (ed.), *Report of the Twenty-Third Annual Round Table Meeting on Linguistics and Language Studies* (Washington, DC, 1973), pp. 273–87.

[32] F. DE SAUSSURE, *Cours de linguistique générale*, 5th edn (Paris, 1955).

[33] U. WEINREICH, W. LABOV and M. I. HERZOG, 'Empirical foundations for a theory of language change', in W. P. Lehmann and Y. Malkiel (eds), *Directions for Historical Linguistics* (Austin, Texas, 1968), pp. 95–195.

[34] L. WITTGENSTEIN, *Philosophical Investigations*, trans. G. E. M. Anscombe (Oxford, 1953).

[35] W. LABOV, 'Contraction, deletion, and inherent variability of the English copula', *Language*, vol. 45 (1969), pp. 715–62.

[36] W. WOLFRAM, *Sociolinguistic Aspects of Assimilation: Puerto Rican English in New York City* (Arlington, 1974).

[37] H. CEDERGREN and D. SANKOFF, 'Variable rules: performance as a statistical reflection of competence', *Language*, vol. 50 (1974), pp. 333–55.

[38] W. LABOV, *The Social Stratification of English in New York City* (Washington, DC, 1966).

[39] P. TRUDGILL, *The Social Differentiation of English in Norwich* (Cambridge, 1974).

[40] P. TRUDGILL, 'Phonological rules and sociolinguistic variation in Norwich English', in C.-J. N. Bailey and R. W. Shuy (eds), *New Ways of Analysing Variation in English* (Washington, DC, 1973), pp. 149–63.

[41] N. CHOMSKY, 'Knowledge of language', in K. Gunderson (ed.), *Language, Mind, and Knowledge* (Minneapolis, 1975), pp. 299–320.

[42] W. WÖLCK, *Phonematische Analyse der Sprache von Buchan* (Heidelberg, 1965).

[43] D. BICKERTON, *Dynamics of a Creole System* (Cambridge, 1975).

[44] P. H. MATTHEWS, review of Brown [25], *Journal of Linguistics*, vol. 11 (1975), pp. 322–43.

[45] N. CHOMSKY, 'The formal nature of language', in E. H. Lenneberg, *Biological Foundations of Language* (New York, 1967), pp. 397–442.

[46] N. CHOMSKY, *Language and Mind*, 2nd edn (New York, 1972).

[47] J. J. KATZ and J. A. FODOR, 'The structure of a semantic theory', *Language*, vol. 39 (1963), pp. 170–210.

[48] D. L. BOLINGER, 'The atomization of meaning', *Language*, vol. 41 (1965), pp. 555–73.

[49] G. LAKOFF, 'Hedges: a study in meaning criteria and the logic of fuzzy concepts', *Papers from the Eighth Regional Meeting, Chicago Linguistic Society* (1972), pp. 183–228.

[50] G. MOUNIN, *Les problèmes théoriques de la traduction* (Paris, 1963).

[51] C. E. BAZELL, 'The correspondence fallacy in structural linguistics', reprinted in E. P. Hamp, F. W. Householder and R. Austerlitz (eds), *Readings in Linguistics II* (Chicago, 1966), pp. 271–98.

[52] A. J. GREIMAS, *Sémantique structurale* (Paris, 1966).

[53] K. BALDINGER, *Teoría semántica* (Madrid, 1970).

[54] J. J. KATZ and T. G. BEVER, 'The fall and rise of empiricism', in T. G. Bever, J. J. Katz and D. T. Langendoen (eds), *An Integrated Theory of Linguistic Ability* (Hassocks, 1977), pp. 11–64.

[55] W. L. CHAFE, *Meaning and the Structure of Language* (Chicago, 1970).

[56] R. W. LANGACKER, *Language and its Structure* (New York, 1968).

[57] J. R. ROSS, 'On declarative sentences', in R. A. Jacobs and P. S. Rosenbaum (eds), *Readings in English Transformational Grammar* (Waltham, Mass., 1970), pp. 222–72.

[58] P. H. MATTHEWS, review of Jacobs and Rosenbaum, *Readings in English Transformational Grammar*, in *Journal of Linguistics*, vol. 8 (1972), pp. 125–36.

[59] RUTH M. KEMPSON, *Presupposition and the Delimitation of Semantics* (Cambridge, 1975).

[60] A. H. GARDINER, *The Theory of Speech and Language*, 2nd edn (Oxford, 1951).

[61] J. M. SADOCK, *Toward a Linguistic Theory of Speech Acts* (New York, 1974).

[62] P. H. MATTHEWS, review of Sadock [61], *General Linguistics*, vol. 16 (1976), pp. 236–42.

[63] N. CHOMSKY, 'Deep structure, surface structure, and semantic interpretation', in D. D. Steinberg and L. A. Jakobovits (eds), *Semantics* (Cambridge, 1971), pp. 183–216.

[64] N. CHOMSKY, 'Form and meaning in natural languages', in Chomsky [46], pp. 100–14.

[65] P. F. STRAWSON, 'Meaning and truth', in *Logico-Linguistic Papers* (London, 1971), pp. 170–89.

[66] W. HAAS, 'Meaning and rules', *Proceedings of the Aristotelian Society*, n.s., vol. 73 (1972/3), pp. 135–55.

[67] H. W. FOWLER, *A Dictionary of Modern English Usage* (Oxford, 1926).

[68] C. E. BAZELL, 'Three misconceptions of grammaticalness', in C. I. J. M. Stuart (ed.), *Report of the Fifteenth Annual (First International) Round Table Meeting on Linguistics and Language Studies* (Washington, DC, 1964), pp. 3–9.

[69] D. L. BOLINGER, 'Syntactic blends and other matters', *Language*, vol. 37 (1961), pp. 366–81.

[70] F. R. PALMER, 'Noun-phrase and sentence: a problem in semantics/syntax', *Transactions of the Philological Society*, 1972, pp. 20–43.

[71] N. RUWET, 'La syntaxe du pronom "en" et la transformation de "montée du sujet" ', in *Théorie syntaxique et syntaxe du français* (Paris, 1972), pp. 48–86.

[72] J. PIAGET, *Biologie et connaissance* (Paris, 1967).

[73] L. BLOOMFIELD, *Language,* English edn (London, 1935).

[74] Z. S. HARRIS, *Methods in Structural Linguistics* (Chicago, 1951).

[75] L. BLOOMFIELD, review of J. Ries, *Was ist ein Satz?* (Prague, 1931), in C. F. Hockett (ed.), *A Leonard Bloomfield Anthology* (Bloomington, 1970), pp. 231–6.

[76] G. RYLE, *The Concept of Mind* (London, 1949).

[77] 'Gesprekken met Noam Avram Chomsky', *Vrij Nederland,* 14 January 1978.

INDEX

Numbers refer to sections